Bayou Built

The Legacy of Louisiana's Historic Architecture

Peter Mires

iUniverse, Inc.
New York   Bloomington

Bayou Built
The Legacy of Louisiana's Historic Architecture

The views expressed in this work are solely those of the author and do not necessarily reflect the views of the publisher, and the publisher hereby disclaims any responsibility for them.

iUniverse books may be ordered through booksellers or by contacting:

iUniverse
1663 Liberty Drive
Bloomington, IN 47403
www.iuniverse.com
1-800-Authors (1-800-288-4677)

Because of the dynamic nature of the Internet, any Web addresses or links contained in this book may have changed since publication and may no longer be valid.

ISBN: 978-1-4502-6367-2 (sc)
ISBN: 978-1-4502-6368-9 (ebk)

Printed in the United States of America

iUniverse rev. date: 10/25/2010

Contents

Preface

I am a geographer, and Fall Semester 2005 I was teaching a course entitled Online Weather Studies. On Saturday, August 27 at 5:16 a.m. (I do my best work at this time of day thanks to French roast coffee) I sent the following E-mail to my students.

> If you've been watching The Weather Channel, you know that Katrina passed over south Florida and is now strengthening in the Gulf of Mexico. The projected path is the central Gulf, and the city of New Orleans is getting worried. I lived in south Louisiana (Baton Rouge) for six years, and I know that meteorologists have said for a long time that New Orleans is a disaster waiting to happen. Much of the city is below sea level and there are essentially only three ways out of the city: I-10 east, I-10 west, and north across Lake Pontchartrain. This is worth keeping a close eye on (no pun intended). When you go to the National Hurricane Center's web site, click on the 3-day cone and you'll see what I mean.

As we all know, Hurricane Katrina made landfall on Monday, August 29 with devastating effect. Levees collapsed, Lake Pontchartrain poured in, and the Ninth Ward and much of St. Bernard Parish east of the city went the way of Atlantis. It was our worst fears realized.

Peter Mires

A casualty of Katrina less often mentioned is the Bayou State's historic architecture. I would not suggest that lodging is on par with life and limb, but like most things historic, old houses are non-renewable resources. Although I teach physical science courses like meteorology, I am also a student of the cultural landscape, and the objects of my study have included the historic houses of Louisiana. After seeing images of Hurricane Katrina's devastation on television, I returned to some of my research, including a 1987 report that I had written for the New Orleans District of the U.S. Army Corps of Engineers on the architectural history of Southeast Louisiana. I realized that more than a few of the old folk and vernacular houses south and east of New Orleans—in the parishes of St. Bernard, Plaquemines, and Jefferson—were probably gone.

I belong to an organization called the National Trust for Historic Preservation because I believe that the historic built environment is a legacy that enriches our daily lives, and it is something worthy to pass on to future generations. I like the thought that we can live in layered landscapes where not everything old is bulldozed to make way for the modern. For the past eleven years, for example, my wife and I have been restoring our Gothic Revival Victorian home located in a neighborhood containing houses ranging in age from the 1850s to the townhouses currently under construction down the street. That is why I felt a huge sense of loss from Katrina; aside from lives lost and livelihoods interrupted, many of the old houses from what New Orleans author Harnett T. Kane called the Deep Delta Country will no longer add their unique texture and depth to the landscape.

A lot of people agree with me that we need the past around us for a variety of reasons, not the least of which is that it provides a sense of direction. A teacher of mine once explained that you need at least two points in order to draw a straight line, and, over the years, I have extrapolated that maxim well beyond a simple geometry lesson. It is a lesson that most Louisianians understand and take to heart. The past is a vital part of life in the present; it imparts a sense of continuity and cultural tradition. Old houses great and small can be found throughout the state.

Sometimes preservation in Louisiana has been accomplished by moving a collection of historic standing structures to outdoor rural life museums, such as the one maintained by Louisiana State University in Baton Rouge or "Acadian Village" in Cajun Country outside Lafayette. These places, with their manicured landscapes, abundant signage, and informative docents are interesting and educational, but the buildings have been removed from everyday experience. More incongruous, however, is the *in situ* preservation of some of the incomparable plantation homes along River Road between Baton Rouge and New Orleans. Some of these examples of antebellum architectural grandeur have not been moved from their original site, but instead survive entrapped just feet from a web of horizontal pipes and vertical smokestacks of petroleum and chemical plants found along this stretch of the Mississippi River.

Fortunately, most of the state's remaining historic architecture still retains its contextual integrity. Most old houses have not been moved to an outdoor museum or confined like a ship in a bottle. Various organizations and state agencies, particularly the Louisiana Division of Historic Preservation, have done their part. The National Trust has been caretaker of an elegant plantation home, "Shadows on the Teche" in Iberia Parish, since 1958. However, most of the credit for the survival of Louisiana's historic architecture goes to its citizens, ordinary people who have taken care of their old houses from generation to generation. They have done so because, like me, they identify with the contribution that historic architecture makes to the cultural landscape.

Louisiana is a special place. I discovered that when my parents first took my brother and me to New Orleans in 1962. How incredibly different and exotic it seemed to me, a nine-year-old boy from Delaware. I saw where the pirate Jean Lafitte used to hang out in the French Quarter and imagined myself as Mark Twain on a Mississippi River steamboat. I saw real alligators! My parents used to kid me about how I ducked into some dive on Bourbon Street only to be returned moments later by a chuckling bouncer. There was also the architecture. Although the word *ambience* was not yet part of my vocabulary, I sensed it; wrought iron balconies and old brick and hidden courtyards with banana trees gave the place a special feeling.

Twenty years later I returned to the Bayou State to work on my doctorate in geography at Louisiana State University. Another two decades have passed since that work was completed and I moved off to my first college teaching position. What is it about this span of time that demographers call a generation? Perhaps it is special because it gives us sufficient time to reflect on continuity and change. A few years ago I read *New Orleans, Mon Amour: Twenty Years of Writings from the City* by Andrei Codrescu. He argues that New Orleans (and the state generally) casts a spell. You may leave it, but it never leaves you. I know he speaks the truth; my house is filled with reminders of Louisiana, including souvenirs from that boyhood visit to the Crescent City.

What follows is a perspective on Louisiana's history, culture, and domestic architecture. To gain this perspective it is necessary to appreciate the temporal and spatial contexts of old houses, so more space is devoted to these concerns than is typical of most books on architectural history. Also, this book is about everyday houses. Louisiana is rightfully recognized for its magnificent antebellum plantation homes, and they are discussed here, but as a geographer who has traveled all of the state's sixty-four parishes in search of folk and vernacular houses I realize that those columned mansions are only a small segment of Louisiana's built environment.

A glance at the notes and bibliography in the back of this book will confirm how much I owe a debt to other writers. If I had to identify a single individual for special acknowledgement, it would be the late Dr. Milton B. Newton, Jr. who mentored me in my doctoral studies at LSU. Part of this preface was previously published in the journal *FOCUS on Geography*, and I thank the American Geographical Society for permission to reprint here. Finally, I thank my family, both affineal and consanguineal, for their love and support, with a special thanks to my wife Kimberly. I dedicate this book to the memory of my mother, Ruth Bingham Mires.

Although this is the last sentence in the book to use the first person singular pronoun, I hope that my affection for the state still rebounding from Hurricane Katrina is apparent to even the casual reader.

PM
Laurel, Delaware
October 3, 2010

1. Time, Space, and Houses

The diversity of Louisiana landscapes, both physical and cultural, is part of its appeal. Contrary to its moniker as "The Bayou State," Louisiana's varied environment ranges from pine forests in the north to coastal marshes fringing the Gulf of Mexico, with prairies, swamps, river valleys, and rolling uplands in between. People from other places—French, German, Spanish, British, and African, among others—joined the Native American population to form what many have called a *melange*, or gumbo, of cultures. Their imprint on the land is still apparent in the houses that they built, which, rightfully, have been the subject of numerous books and articles.

The abundant literature on the domestic architecture of Louisiana generally has a focus.[1] A work may be devoted to a particular class, culture, or building material, such as the antebellum plantation home, French Creole vernacular, or Upland South log construction. It may focus on a specific place, such as New Orleans or that aquatic corridor along the Mississippi River known as the River Road. Some books on the subject amount to an architectural history of the state featuring extant examples of various styles. Others incorporate houses, particularly folk houses, into a wider discussion of the cultural landscape. Few, however, address the settlement process, that unique human-environment relationship that explains how this architectural mosaic developed over time.

The settlement of Louisiana can be thought of as a series of kaleidoscopic patterns resulting from more than simple population spread and increase. Economic opportunity and technical innovation played large roles in determining the viability of any part of the state. For example, some areas remained sparsely populated until the introduction of the railroad made feasible the extraction of timber and stimulated the growth of service centers. The same railroad, on the other hand, could spell disaster for the river town whose importance as a point of shipment rapidly declined. These changes should be reflected in the pattern of domestic architecture.

This book is fundamentally a work of historical geography, rather than an architectural history per se. It examines the pattern of Louisiana's historic domestic architecture against the processual backdrop of two centuries of settlement. The goal is to establish a context—a temporal and spatial frame of reference—by which most houses built before the twentieth century may be evaluated. The view taken here is that historic standing structures are artifacts; they are what survive from the past—theoretically, from a pool of every structure ever built. In the aggregate, they form the relict cultural landscape. It is not what remains that is the focus of this book, but the physical and cultural milieu of which these remnants were once a part.

For historical geographers, the settlement of an area is viewed through the dimensions of time and space. Within the temporal dimension, they can limit their observation synchronically, that is the distribution of phenomena at one time, or choose the more ambitious diachronic historical study, attempting to account for change over time.[2] A comprehensive diachronic historical geography is impossible to achieve, so the "time-slice" method serves as a substitute.

The time-slice method involves the sequence of synchronic geographies spaced at intervals covering the desired span of history. The selection of each slice, also called a "stage" or "cross-section," is usually based on its representation of social and technological trends that punctuate history, that which the historian commonly calls periods.[3] In thinking about the time-slice method, it is worthwhile to recall geographer Andrew Clark's comment that, "conditions observed at any period of time are to be understood as momentary states in continuing and complex processes of change."[4] The time-slice, therefore, is a device used to isolate periods of time for the purpose of description and analysis.

Some social scientists prefer to conceive of historical change not merely as a continuum of constant change, but more of a punctuated equilibrium. Certainly, in our long span of recorded history, greatly expanded by prehistorical and paleoanthropological research, we refer to great events such as "the agricultural revolution" and "the industrial revolution." The profound change brought about by some sudden social or technological occurrence or innovation then becomes the accepted mode until replaced or modified by the next punctuation.[5]

American geographers have conceived of historical change as punctuated equilibrium since the 1920s. In Derwent Whittlesey's brief article on the nature of historical geography he advocated a concept of the field as "a succession of *stages* of human occupance."[6] He refers to this succession as sequent occupance.

Sequent occupance has been a useful organizing device for historical geographers since Whittlesey's initial enunciation of the term. The fatal flaw in this model, however, is his assertion that "human occupance of area, like other biotic phenomena, carries within itself the seed of its own transformation." This is a form of intellectual determinism that was quickly rejected. In an insightful analysis of sequent occupance in American geography, Marvin Mikesell argued that its decline resulted from growing dissatisfaction in "an approach that offered effects without causes and demanded acceptance of the premise that process is implicit in stage."[7] Fully cognizant of the pitfalls inherent in sequent occupance, as originally defined, historical geographers have retained the time-slice method as a useful organizational device for the presentation of diachronic geographical data. They also have not neglected to address the question of process.

A concern for the description and analysis of the causal factors of change to complement the time-slice is evident in a study published in the early 1930s. In his historical geography of the Santa Clara Valley of California, Jan Broek linked four time-slice chapters representing the significant periods in the valley's occupation with three intervening chapters dealing with the processes responsible for changes manifested on the landscape.[8] In a later publication, Broek explained his method.[9]

> The somewhat original device I used was to divide the treatment of each period in two parts. The first was explanatory: it analyzed the forces and functions that shaped the mode of life in the valley. The second part described the cultural landscape resulting from the social-economic determinants. In this manner, "process" received due attention, but its scope was guided and restrained by the relevance of its forces to the purpose of this study, namely understanding the landscape.

A similar two-part time-slice method, where each time-slice has a process and a landscape component, is used here. In this case, the settlement process is given considerably more attention than is typical of most books on architectural history. The cultural landscape, mainly in the form of domestic structures, is used as tangible evidence representative of processes such as migration, diffusion, population growth and expansion, and environmental adaptation that characterize each time-slice.

Because settlement was an ongoing process, it is necessary to somehow synthesize or distill this information to make it manageable. And yet, to approximate historical reality the synthesis should not be so generalizing as to obscure or dilute important historical and geographical changes. The selection of each time-slice was done with this in mind, and in terms of both number and spacing they are more than sufficient for the purpose.

Historic Structures as Artifacts

Humankind is not the only species to seek shelter for comfort and protection. We cannot even claim the monopoly on construction. This is readily apparent to anyone who has taken the time to inspect a beaver's house or prairie dog town, for example. Yet, it seems that cross-culturally, and well back into prehistory, ours is a species endowed with a penchant for building. Among the vast variety of constructions that comprise the so-called "built environment," houses are the most fundamental. The need for shelter obviously supercedes the need to build schools, churches, and courthouses. Although civic architecture, such as schools, churches, and courthouses, provide loci for the satisfaction of other human needs—education, worship, and justice—the primacy of housing cannot be overstated.

Early pioneer settings in Louisiana neatly illustrate the importance of shelter. Upon moving into an area, the pioneer's first concern was housing. In many cases, land clearing and house building took place simultaneously. The felled trees in areas of Anglo settlement commonly received minimal modification prior to their use in horizontal log construction. In French-settled Louisiana, timber was hand-hewn for heavy timber-frame construction. Even with the aggregation of individuals into communities, public and commercial buildings were often minimal. Circuit-riding teachers, preachers, and judges served a population dispersed over a vast territory for much of Louisiana's history. Aside from the domicile and its associated buildings, such as barns, corncribs, smokehouses, sheds, and the like, stores may have been the most common structures of the historic built environment. The house, therefore, is the most basic structure of the built environment. With respect to historic constructions on the landscape of Louisiana, houses are, according to geographer Fred Kniffen, "perhaps numerically the most prominent of anything man had done."[10]

Besides being fundamental to humans as basic shelter and numerous and conspicuous on the landscape, houses are items of material culture with attributes of cultural and historical significance beyond the individual specimen. They are artifacts of shared beliefs and values—culture. One merely has to drive through a modern subdivision and observe the uniformity to confirm the "shared" nature of housing. Houses are not idiosyncratic constructions, although some wealthy individuals and innovative architects have deviated significantly from the norm.

It is not only valid, but conceptually useful, to think of houses as artifacts. Anthropologists and cultural geographers have devoted a great deal of study to the ways in which material items manifest the cultures that produce them. Morphological characteristics of items tend to be non-random and reflect cultural choices in such attributes as material, form, decorative treatment, and so forth. The anthropologist James Deetz used the term "mental template" to describe what is considered to be good and proper (culturally acceptable) by those who make and use material items.[11]

> The idea of the proper form of an object exists in the mind of the maker, and when this idea is expressed in tangible form in raw material, an artifact results. The idea is the mental template from which the craftsman makes the object. The form of an artifact is a close approximation of this template, and variations in a group of similar objects reflect variation in the ideas which produce them.

Thus, to a large extent, form follows idea. This idea is essentially bounded by cultural parameters. Where form differs, cultural values and beliefs should theoretically account for the differences. This is the fundamental basis and theoretical justification for the classification of cultural material. It links our observation and description of material items to particular cultures, allowing us to identify them as culture traits. Further, it is the grammar by which we may speak of cultural process.

Typology and Houses

One question that has troubled those who attempt to deal taxonomically with cultural material has been this: Do the types that we establish truly represent, to use Deetz's term, a mental template? In other words, can we really decipher mental template by observation and description, or are types simply imposed by the researcher to facilitate the study of cultural material?[12]

Cultural geographers, most notably Fred Kniffen, have used typology as a descriptive and analytic tool. It has been applied with greatest frequency and success to houses, although other forms on the cultural landscape, such as fences, fields, survey systems, and cemeteries have also been subject to typological consideration. Their involvement in typological studies can be traced directly to Kniffen's seminal 1936 article on Louisiana house types.[13]

There has been a cross-fertilization of ideas on the nature of typology between the disciplines of anthropology and geography. It is not surprising that James Ford used house types as illustrations in his article "The Type Concept Revisited."[14] He expressed a keen interest in Kniffen's work on Louisiana house types. In fact, he made the drawings of house types for Kniffen's 1936 article. At the same time, Kniffen kept close ties with archaeologists such as Ford and their typological efforts, particularly with prehistoric ceramics.[15]

The issue of whether we can discover the mental template through typology will probably never be fully resolved. Nevertheless, we continue to use it successfully as a descriptive and analytic tool, and frequently make the assumption that our constructs approximate past reality. We realize that typologies often create ideal types out of composite attributes, and few, if any, actual specimens match the specifications of the type. The term "sameness-in-diversity" neatly sums up the purpose of typology, and abstract thought generally.[16]

Houses in Time and Space

Those who study material culture do so within the dimensions of time and space. This is usually accomplished through a considerable amount of field observation and careful description, leading to the establishment of types. Then, distribution studies placing the types in their temporal and spatial contexts may allow for higher-level theoretical considerations. Such cultural processes as diffusion or migration, for example, can be postulated only by beginning with the fundamental abstraction of type.

Just about anything classified—things having a distribution—exist within temporal and spatial dimensions, and archaeologists, for example, use the concepts of "tradition" and "horizon" to define those relationships. Tradition, according to archaeologists Gordon Willey and Philip Phillips, is defined as, "temporal continuity represented by persistent configurations in single technologies or other systems of related forms."[17] They define horizon, on the other hand, as, "a primarily spatial continuity represented by cultural traits and assemblages whose nature and mode of occurrence permit the assumption of a broad and rapid spread."[18] The implication of this conceptual framework for the built environment is, simply, that except for the completely idiosyncratic, structures have important linkages to other structures in both time and space.

Another important and related concept is that of change over time and through space. Morphological change may appear to be genetic, that is to behave biologically. This is, however, a distortion of the nature of culture change. Forms are frequently said to "evolve" out of other forms. Hybridization, biological distance, and isolation are common concepts often used to explain the unique and different.

Change in material culture does not occur as a function of time, space, or culture contact per se; morphological modification results from the deliberate decisions of people. Forms may be seen to change through time, but time does not cause change. Likewise, there may be continuity or change in material culture over space, but there is no equation governing change because of linear distance or environment. Finally, culture contact situations do not necessarily insure change. Introduction of an innovation is still subject to cultural acceptance or rejection.

The placement of types in the temporal dimension is done by either relative or absolute dating methods. Relative dating is a system of "ordinal" classification independent of reference to a specific calendar year. It is frequently used in the ordering of an assemblage of archaeological artifacts. In the nineteenth century, the curator of the Danish National Museum in Copenhagen, for example, was challenged to categorize and display a large group of artifacts his museum had acquired from all over Europe, and he devised one of the most familiar examples of relative dating. C.J. Thomsen was aware that ancient tools composed of different materials were unearthed at different levels, and the three-age system—stone, bronze, and iron—was born.[19]

Houses are relatively dated in several ways. A single structure may exhibit several phases of construction and may be ordered accordingly. Elements of architectural style with a temporal range of popularity may be present. Methods of construction and material may help bracket a date range for probable date of construction. Documentary records may help isolate a probable date of construction. Datable archaeological material may be found in and around the structure. Finally, a house may be dated relatively by comparison with similar structures of known age.

Absolute dating of a structure means that a specific calendar year for the date of construction is known or discoverable. A structure's absolute date of construction may be recorded: 1) in documentary sources; 2) on the building itself in the form of an inscription; 3) by informants; and 4) by material for which an absolute date is obtainable, for example with wood datable by means of dendrochronology.

Those who study old houses often use relative dating when evaluating the changes a house has undergone in the form of additions and alterations. It is possible to examine structural and stylistic differences evident in a single structure and to order them chronologically in relative terms. A good example of this comes from what is now the Pointe Coupee Parish Museum near New Roads, Louisiana (Figure 1). The "core" of the house is of planked horizontal log construction with full dovetail corner notching. The chimney divides its two rooms. The addition is of heavy timber construction filled with mud and moss, known locally by the French term *bousillage*. The dates of construction for both the core and the addition are not known. However, we may confidently speak of this structure in relative terms; the left side, facing the structure, is earlier than the right.

Figure 1. Pointe Coupee Parish Museum. Photograph by the author.

Another example of the relative dating of a structure comes from the vicinity of Bayou Goula, Iberville Parish. One home, "The Oaks," is distinguished by its two distinct components (Figure 2). The right half, facing the structure, is the original part. It is a typical smaller Creole house. The repaired roof covers the former location of a central chimney. The left half is the addition. Both structurally and stylistically it is typical of a Queen Anne Victorian house. In this case, the family lived initially in the Creole house, but when eventually they could afford to expand, did so according to the dictates of contemporary fashion.

Figure 2. "The Oaks," Iberville Parish. Photograph by the author.

Relative dating by stylistic means is accomplished by identifying elements of an architectural style and assigning a date based on the temporal range of that style's popularity.[20] There are at least three major considerations when attempting to date by style: 1) many houses, especially folk and vernacular houses, display few or no attributes of architectural style; 2) attributes of architectural style may be added or removed; and 3) more than one style may be present.

A house without architectural style may seem impossible to some, but style, by definition, is not necessarily an integral structural component. According to the *Oxford English Dictionary*, style is "a definite type of architecture, distinguished by special characteristics of structure or ornamentation."[21] Husband and wife architectural historians Lee and Virginia McAlester make the distinction between folk houses and "styled" houses.[22]

Domestic buildings are of two principal sorts: folk houses and styled houses. Folk houses are those designed without a conscious attempt to mimic current fashion. Many are built by their occupants or by non-professional builders, and all are relatively simple houses meant to provide basic shelter, with little concern for presenting a stylish face to the world.

Style, according to geographer Milton Newton, "amounts to fashion or fad."[23] This form of embellishment is frequently absent in folk housing. The authors of a National Trust for Historic Preservation publication underscore this point. According to their definition, style "is essentially visual and has no necessary relationship to the function of the building."[24]

Stylistic elements may be added or removed according to current fashion. Geographers Richard Pillsbury and Andrew Kardos liken style to clothing: "Style is like clothing on a house, easily altered to meet the fashions of the times with little real impact on the contents inside."[25] Dell Upton and John Vlach, specialists in vernacular architecture, relate the old story of a man "who put up a building, then went to the lumberyard to buy some *architecture* to nail onto it."[26] Lee and Virginia McAlester correlate the popularity of adding stylistic elements to a folk house with the transportation revolution begun by the railroads.[27]

> The growth of the railroad system made heavy woodworking machinery widely accessible at local trade centers, where they produced inexpensive Victorian detailing. The railroads also provided local lumber yards with abundant supplies of pre-cut detailing from distant mills. Many builders simply grafted pieces of this newly available trim onto the traditional folk house forms familiar to local carpenters. Fashion-conscious homeowners also updated their older folk houses with new Victorian porches.

The man who went to the lumberyard to buy "architecture" was really purchasing architectural style!

Because of a homeowner's desire to keep up with current fashion and to demonstrate "good taste," many houses display elements of more than one architectural style. This could result from a house being built during periods of stylistic transition or when different styles competed for popularity. Intermittent attempts at keeping an older house in step with stylistic fashion could also produce a house displaying more than one architectural style.

Method of construction and material may provide clues as to the probable age of a structure. Some notable examples with temporal significance include method of wall construction, especially balloon framing indicating a post-1850 structure, lumber milling, and nail type.[28] These features, among others, pertain to the fundamental structure of the house and should serve as a reliable means of relative dating. Although recycling of older material such as sash-sawn lumber and machine-cut nails has been known to occur, it is usually possible to distinguish curation behavior from original structure based on other contextual information. Conversely, newer material such as aluminum siding is often added to an older structure.

Documents, both written and graphic, can yield a relative date for a structure. Written information such as wills, diaries, ledgers, tax records, newspaper accounts, and local histories frequently mention specific structures, thus providing a *terminus ante quem*, or "date before which" the house must have been built.

Cartographic sources, notably the Sanborn Fire Insurance Company maps, often show structures in scaled ground plan. They have been used successfully by cultural geographers studying old buildings. A structure with matching location and ground plan is, in all likelihood, the same structure. Old photographs, sketches, and drawings in which the structure appears also can aid in relative dating.

Historic structures can be dated through archaeological methods. This usually entails subsurface examination underneath, adjacent to, and in the vicinity of the historic structure. This relative dating technique involves, among other things, the location of refuse disposal areas and the excavation of builder's trenches.

Analogy is perhaps the most common relative dating technique. Archaeologists use it constantly. Rather than having to date each and every item, they assume that formal similarity denotes coevality. Those who study houses work under the same basic assumption, as do other specialists such as paleontologists and art historians.

The date of construction for most plantation homes in Louisiana is generally a relative date. Even great homes on the National Register of Historic Places, for example Parlange in Pointe Coupee Parish, are dated relatively. Their date of construction is often preceded by "circa." More modest houses—older folk and vernacular—are almost always relatively dated. Absolute dates, however, are occasionally obtainable.

Documents, such as those mentioned above, may well specify a date of construction. These can be somewhat deceptive or vague. The terms "early," "mid" (or "middle"), and "late" are indicative of relative dating. Authors of local histories are particularly fond of stating dates in this manner. It is a relative date the same as a date preceded by "circa."

Occasionally an absolute date will be assigned to a house that little deserves it. There have been instances of older houses burning down practically to the foundations and then being essentially rebuilt. The distinction between "restoration" and "reconstruction" has long plagued preservationists. Often there are various interpretations of these terms. Obviously, old foundations do not always an old house make.

In rare cases an absolute date is inscribed on or within the structure. This is much more common with civic architecture, but there are instances of an artisan inscribing his initials and a date on the wooden framing of a house. For example, the date 1852 appears on the cornice of "The Armitage" in Terrebonne Parish.[29]

Informants can sometimes supply an absolute date for the construction of a house. This is particularly true of houses built in the latter half of the twentieth century. On occasion, the resident is the builder. Residents sometimes retain documents of rich historical value that go beyond providing an absolute date of construction. In 1984, the author encountered an old storekeeper who was able to produce the bill of sale for the lumber that was used to build the store.[30] His father purchased it from the Whitecastle Lumber and Shingle Company for $128.00, and the bill was dated March 6, 1890.

An effective, albeit infrequently used, method of obtaining an absolute date of construction for a wooden house is dendrochronology, or tree-ring dating. It has been used with some degree of success in other areas of the Southeastern United States and wooden structures in Louisiana, particularly those made of bald cypress, can easily be tied to a greater regional chronology.[31]

The spatial dimension of house types derives from the movement of people holding distinctive building traditions, the imprint of these traditions on the landscape, and the general spread of ideas concerning housing. Although the migrations of people and the diffusion of ideas have an undeniable temporal component, the cultural manifestations of these processes are also observable areal associations.

Migration and Cultural Influences

Louisiana has received repeated waves of migrants and immigrants with differing cultural backgrounds over the course of three hundred years of settlement. Along with other beliefs, values, and practices, each group brought its building traditions. Some of these have become part of the cultural landscape of today.

While most of these groups maintained their cultural identities and expressed them through the houses that they built, two processes—assimilation and syncretism—have blurred traditional forms. Some ethnic groups have come to Louisiana and totally assimilated with respect to the material culture of the local, dominant group. For example, large numbers of Germans immigrated to Louisiana in 1720s and 1730s and settled up river from New Orleans in St. Charles and St. John the Baptist parishes. They adopted the traditional building methods of their French neighbors to the degree that they are indistinguishable.

A syncretism, or blending, of building attributes has also taken place here in Louisiana. The best example of this is what is known as the Louisiana Creole house. It seems to be a composite structure with building elements traceable to three continents.

Building Traditions

Cultural geographers recognize four separate building traditions in Louisiana folk housing. They are the pen tradition, the French tradition, the shotgun tradition, and the pyramidal tradition.[32] Of these, the first two have the greatest distribution. They represent the great cultural dichotomy of the Bayou State: Anglo-American and French. The shotgun tradition is somewhat controversial as to origins, but it is neither Anglo-American nor French exclusively. The pyramidal tradition is associated with the late nineteenth century railroad and lumber boom.

The French and various subsets of the Anglo-American building traditions in Louisiana display some well-defined distributions. The Upland South variant predominates in the hill and terrace regions of North Louisiana and the Florida Parishes. The Lowland South variant in Louisiana is confined to the major waterways with significant alluvial floodplains. A late arrival, and subset of the greater Anglo-American tradition, the Midwest I-house, is concentrated in the prairies of Southwestern Louisiana. Additionally, the French building tradition generally occurs south of a line running from the mouth of the Sabine River to Avoyelles Parish to Lake Borgne. It also extends up the Red River as far as Natchitoches Parish.

The pen tradition comes directly from the British Isles and is essentially a modular form of construction. The basic building unit is the pen, also called a bay. It is sometimes square, but more often rectangular. The most common pen sizes are a square measuring sixteen by sixteen feet or a rectangle sixteen by eighteen feet.[33] The simplest house consists of a single pen with gable roof, chimney at one gable end, and entrances on each of the eave sides.

Houses all across British-settled northeastern North America employed the pen tradition as the basic module, and in expansion. In all three regional culture hearths—New England, the Middle Atlantic, and Tidewater Virginia—different house types arose out of this shared building tradition. Three subsets of this tradition are important to the cultural landscape of Louisiana: Upland South houses, Lowland South houses, and I-houses.

A distinctive set of traits fused in the southern Appalachians in the late eighteenth and early nineteenth centuries to form what is called the Upland South culture. The people were mainly of German and Scotch-Irish ancestry. They were the pioneers of lore. After immigrating largely to the middle colonies of the Eastern Seaboard, they quickly moved beyond the settled coastal plain and pushed into the frontier south and west of the Appalachians. They brought with them a mental template of the house types of the Middle Atlantic region and knowledge of horizontal log construction.[34]

The lowland South culture came to Louisiana from the Tidewater region of Virginia and the Carolinas. These people were strongly British in ancestry and custom, and geared to a plantation economy. Tidewater Virginia, after all, is where the plantation system began in British North America. They moved directly to Louisiana and transplanted their cultural traditions in areas suitable for plantation agriculture. Kniffen described this transplantation as a movement from Tidewater Virginia of "aristocratic planters thoroughly imbued with ideas as to the proper manner of living and equipped with the capital and slave labor sufficient to put them into effect."[35] Although far fewer Lowland South whites than Upland South people came to Louisiana, their building traditions are present, nonetheless, on the cultural landscape.

A house type more closely affiliated with the Upland South, but not belonging to its building traditions exclusively is the I-house. Kniffen named this family of related forms the "I-house" because of its almost total dominance as the apotheosis of a farm house in the states of Indiana, Illinois, and Iowa.[36] Its origin in this country, however, seems to be in the Middle Atlantic region. According to Newton, "I-houses were built in Louisiana from about 1800 until perhaps 1930 in any region where uplanders of plantation background settled, where farmers prospered, or where town dwellers sought to imitate planters."[37]

The French building tradition in Louisiana resembles that of the mother country and the sister colony of French Canada, but is most closely associated with the French Caribbean. This tradition includes heavy timber frame construction filled with brick or mud and moss, a variety of floor plans, steeply pitched side-gabled or hipped roof, frequent use of small dormers, and interior chimney location. The traits acquired from the Caribbean include the raising of the house on a brick basement or posts, broad galleries, often on all four sides, under a continual-pitch or broken-pitch roof, numerous full-length double doors, and outside stairs leading both to the main floor and the loft.

The influence of the Caribbean experience on the building traditions of Louisiana is well documented, but some scholars explain Louisiana French house types in terms of either continental antecedent or indigenous development. Historian Robert Heck, for example, wrote that the Creole house resulted not from contact with planters in the French Caribbean, but because of the Acadians' "sensitivity and acute awareness to the new region [that] encouraged a fuller consciousness of climate, indigenous materials and variations on constructional methods."[38] This explanation ignores the fact that the Creole house was already part of the cultural landscape by the time the Acadians arrived in Louisiana. As Newton points out, "these Caribbean houses had appeared in rural Louisiana by at least 1740, first with planters who emigrated directly from the Caribbean. By the time that Acadians began arriving (1765), the most prestigious form of house was that of the Caribbean planter."[39] Louisiana Creole houses are part of a wider circum-Caribbean family of house types. Even the British raised cottage and the raising of the Upland South types are part of the wider pattern.

The shotgun tradition seems to be a Haitian, and ultimately African, contribution to the Louisiana cultural landscape. The most distinctive feature of houses belonging to this tradition is the location of the entrance at the narrower gable end. Both British and French traditions place the entrance along the wider side. Various explanations have been offered to account for the origin of this tradition, which are neatly summed up by Newton.[40]

> The origin of the shotgun is difficult or impossible to trace. Its origin has been attributed to Louisiana Indian palmetto-covered cabins, to slave memory of a West African house, to houseboats placed on land, to European waterfront settlements, to factory manufacturers of ready-built houses, to the influence of narrow urban lots, and to the Greek Revival fashion.

Although no single explanation seems likely for the source of this building tradition, most scholars favor an African connection.

Finally, the pyramidal tradition is composed of houses displaying a pyramidal roof form. These houses are generally associated with the railroad and lumber boom of the late nineteenth century.

Settlement of the Bayou State

Although human settlement of Louisiana began during the Pleistocene Ice Age some ten thousand years ago and continues with people re-inhabiting places like St. Bernard Parish and the city of New Orleans in the wake of Hurricane Katrina, the imprint of the cultural landscape is best defined by two centuries. The period from the first French settlement on the Gulf Coast in 1699 until the so-called railroad and lumber boom of the 1890s effectively brackets most of what we associate with Louisiana's architectural heritage.

From the perspective of geography the most significant break in the history of settlement of Louisiana was the Louisiana Purchase. Certainly other events, such as the Civil War, had a profound geographical impact, but in the creation of the cultural landscape the eighteenth century was markedly different from the nineteenth century. The Louisiana Purchase in 1803 was significant insofar as it stimulated considerable changes in the settlement pattern that had existed since early French colonial times. From the standpoint of the cultural landscape, these changing patterns are attributed to the influx of settlers with different cultural values. Although Louisiana's Latin roots remain visible and viable to this day, the addition of a formative "American" culture changed the complexion of the place early in the nineteenth century.

While avoiding the pitfalls of environmental determinism, the settlement of Louisiana can be explained, in part, in terms of the exploitation of specific environmental zones. The various cultures that occupied Louisiana in the eighteenth and nineteenth centuries made decisions on site selection based on their intended use of the land and water. Suitability of the land for commercial or subsistence agriculture, logging, or other economic activities, all of which promoted settlement, was a cultural assessment based on physical qualities, such as soil fertility, and cultural considerations, such as accessibility by steamboat.

Transportation played a key role in the settlement, growth, and economic prosperity of Louisiana. During the two centuries examined in this book, residents of Louisiana relied on three principal modes of transport: waterways, roads, and railroads. Any map of colonial land claims attests to the importance of waterways in the settlement of Louisiana. These were threads around which settlement crystallized. Roads have traversed the Louisiana landscape since prehistoric times, and have ranged from ephemeral footpaths to well-traveled thoroughfares. The famous *camino real*, the main route between colonial Louisiana and New Spain, is an example of the latter. The influence of railroads on settlement was overwhelming in some areas of the state during the last three decades of the nineteenth century. Much of North and Southwest Louisiana, for example, experienced unparalleled population expansion in response to the coming of the railroad. The Illinois Central Railroad was actually responsible for the creation of one Louisiana parish; the configuration of Tangipahoa Parish, in fact, appears like a wide right-of-way for the railroad itself.

The settlement of Louisiana from most of the colonial and territorial periods actually took place in specific environments. For a variety of reasons, which mostly concerned agriculture and transportation, settlement concentrated in the bottomlands and blufflands of South Louisiana. Some settlers ventured out into the eastern margins of the prairies in the southwestern portion of the state. The marsh and swamp were strictly avoided for settlement, although resources from these environments were used. The piney woods were sparsely populated throughout the colonial periods, and thinly and unevenly settled in the territorial period.

From the formation of the colony until the end of the territorial period, population clustered in New Orleans and intensified in some specific areas, mainly in the "River Parishes" of South Louisiana. Most of the population inhabited a limited portion of the state, a demographic pattern that would not change until later in the nineteenth century. These areas were, specifically, along the Mississippi from St. Francisville to just below New Orleans, along the upper Lafourche and Teche, around False River in Pointe Coupee Parish, and up the Red as far as Natchitoches.

Census figures clearly indicate nodes of population in incipient towns such as Natchez, later part of the State of Mississippi, Natchitoches, Opelousas, St. Martinville, and Baton Rouge, but New Orleans was the primate, and only, city. Even New Orleans was a relatively small place until the Louisiana Purchase; the population burgeoned after 1803. Urbanization, in the true sense of the term, was not a feature of any other town throughout the colonial and territorial periods.

The ethnicity of the population during the colonial and territorial periods was predominantly French and black African. Germans, Spanish, British, and later Americans added to the ethnic mix. An early geographical pattern developed where the French population became entrenched in the areas of initial occupation. Most blacks were slaves and their presence was greatest in the areas of plantation agriculture. Germans and Spanish settlers tended to assimilate into the dominant French culture. The British occupied the western Florida Parishes. Americans, an admittedly heterogeneous group, arrived in large numbers following the Louisiana Purchase.

Agriculture characterized the economy of the colonial and territorial periods. Most was associated with the plantation system, either directly or indirectly, although independent yeoman farmers engaged in what may fairly be termed subsistence agriculture. Some ranching was also practiced, especially on the prairies near Opelousas and in the Natchitoches area.

Transportation in Louisiana during the colonial and territorial periods was mainly in the form of non-motorized watercraft (the steamboat came later in the nineteenth century) along the state's many navigable waterways. Louisiana's rivers and bayous saw everything from ocean-going sailing ships to small canoe-like *pirogues*. The most common modes of cargo transportation on the Mississippi River were the keelboat and flatboat. Roads were generally bad, but several important routes existed; one significant road was the *camino real*, which began in Natchitoches and had as its southern terminus the capital of New Spain, Mexico City. Louisianians and their goods, however, generally traveled by water.

The architecture of the colonial and territorial periods is predominately French. British Lowland South structures were built to some extent in the Florida Parishes and along the Mississippi. Some Upland South architecture began infiltrating the state during the territorial period, and some initial American architectural influence can be seen in New Orleans in the first decade of the nineteenth century. It is also possible that some African architecture, other than houses belonging to the shotgun tradition, was built in Louisiana at some time during the colonial and territorial periods.[41]

The statehood settlement of Louisiana in the nineteenth century is characterized by a continued growth in the lower alluvial valleys and an expansion into areas that had only been sparsely settled in earlier periods, specifically the piney woods and prairies. The four time-slices of this larger period all highlight the growing importance of the northern half of the state. And, initial occupation of the western and southwestern portions of the state did not take place to any great extent until the 1890s. The environmental component, therefore, can be characterized by widening adaptation and settlement. However, these additional environments do not include the marsh and cypress forests as suitable settlement sites.

Population during statehood grew rapidly, except for the period of the Civil War and Reconstruction. Loss of life during the war, a reduction of immigration, and some emigration combined to produce a plateau in the otherwise ascending trajectory of the state's population. The general pattern of statehood population growth, which actually began during the territorial period, is in stark contrast to the relatively slow population increase of colonial times. Urbanization did not occur to a great degree outside of New Orleans for most of the nineteenth century. Cotton stimulated the growth of some towns such as Shreveport and Monroe, as well as Natchez, Mississippi, late in the antebellum period, but Louisiana was still an agrarian society with a large percentage of the population living in a rural context. The railroad and lumber boom beginning in the 1890s probably did more to stimulate the growth of towns and cities than any other period of settlement. Nevertheless, urbanization was an increasingly important factor in settlement during statehood.

The ethnic composition of Louisiana changed during statehood with the important addition of large numbers of Anglo-Americans. Frenchmen and blacks continued to dominate in the core areas of colonial settlement. Migration of former residents of the East Coast followed. The last migration of the nineteenth century consisted of Northern loggers and Midwestern farmers. These Anglo-Americans tended to settle on the periphery of the famous French triangle, which is defined by corners at New Orleans, Marksville, and Lake Charles.[42]

Although the economies of both the colonial/territorial period and the statehood period were fundamentally agricultural, the statehood period witnessed considerable expansion and change. Cotton was planted in portions of the state's piney woods during the first half of the nineteenth century. Following the Civil War tenant farming kept the plantation system alive. And, the southwestern prairie became a great rice-producing region beginning around 1890.

Transportation was revolutionized during the statehood period, first with the introduction of the steamboat in the second decade of the nineteenth century, and then with the spread of the railroad in the decades following the Civil War. The importance of transportation to the increased distribution of the state's population cannot be overemphasized. The steamboat did for cotton what the railroad later did for industrial lumbering, and it seems that prosperity occurred in proportion to increasingly efficient transportation.

The hallmark of architecture of the statehood period is its "Americanization." Louisiana began to look less like the French Caribbean and more like surrounding Southern states. This was manifested in both house type and architectural style. Architectural style, in fact, became increasingly important for domestic structures though the nineteenth century. French structures continued to be built in the French core, and even adapted architecturally to changes sweeping the rest of the state. Americanization, however, characterized most of Louisiana's architecture for most of the nineteenth century.

Organization of this Book

The rich architectural heritage of the Bayou State is based on structural forms and stylistic elements popular in the eighteenth and nineteenth centuries, and how this built environment became implanted upon the cultural landscape is associated with the process of settlement. This book, therefore, examines both pattern and process. Unlike many books on the architectural history of a place or region, a considerable emphasis is placed on historical and geographical context. Each of the seven chapters begins with a "snap-shot" of the settlement geography of Louisiana at that particular time. Building upon this temporal and spatial framework, characteristics of Louisiana's historic standing houses are presented.

The French colonial period is examined around the year 1740. Technically, the French administered this place named for King Louis XIV from La Salle's "discovery" of the mouth of the Mississippi River in 1682 until the Treaty of Paris in 1763. The year 1775 captures the joint administrations of both Spain and Britain. Louisiana's beginning as a territory of the United States was somewhat politically complex. Spain "retroceded" their portion to Napoleon by secret treaty in 1800, and it was France, not Spain, who sold Louisiana to the United States in that great land deal of 1803. The West Florida Parishes of Louisiana remained Spanish until a rebellion in 1810, when for a brief time an independent Republic of West Florida existed before the United States took political control. The settlement geography and built environment of Territorial Louisiana is portrayed in the year 1810. Four additional "time-slices"—1830, 1850, 1870, and 1890—cover the nineteenth century changes that the State of Louisiana experienced. These correspond to alternating decennial census years, and, significantly, they examine the state during recognized historical periods reflected in changes in the cultural landscape.

2. Environmental Diversity in the Bayou State

This chapter outlines the importance of two environmental characteristics of Louisiana—vegetation and rivers—that compose the physical landscape. Understanding their composition and distribution is, in a very real sense, key to the geographer's agenda. That agenda, simply stated, is the "why" of "where." To know and appreciate the heterogeneous nature of Louisiana's environments is vital to any narrative of its settlement history.

Potential Natural Vegetation

Vegetation, taken as the composite of the whole assemblage of plants growing in an area, responds to such physical environmental factors as climate, soils, hydrology, and elevation. For that reason, natural vegetation provides a good summary indicator of the physical properties of any location. This book uses potential natural vegetation for that purpose. The word "potential" is used here in the same sense that geographer A.W. Kuchler used it in his map *Potential Natural Vegetation of the Coterminous United States*.[1] It is meant to distinguish the vegetational climax communities of the state from the vegetational composition and distribution as seen at present.

The information on Louisiana's potential natural vegetation presented here comes primarily from two sources: the 1937 *Natural Vegetation Map of Louisiana* prepared by the State Board of Engineers, which, in turn, is based on the work of Samuel Lockett, a West Point-trained engineer and Louisiana State University's first geographer.[2] Lockett's 1873 map, in fact, is the first topographical map of the state and the foundation of numerous published maps of the state's potential natural vegetation.[3] In addition to these sources, a map published by the Louisiana Department of Wildlife and Fisheries, *Vegetative Type Map of the Louisiana Coastal Marshes*, has helped clarify the distribution of different marsh communities.[4]

The author has published elsewhere a map of potential natural vegetation as a compilation of the above-mentioned sources.[5] This information was transferred to a series of large-scale maps of Louisiana and converted into digital form suitable for computer cartographic manipulation. The reason for doing so was not simply to produce a sharper image of the state's vegetation; using a geographic information system (GIS) allowed several variables pertaining to the state's settlement history to be compared analytically. In the days prior to GIS, researchers interested in looking at the relationship between two or more variables would display mapped data on transparent sheets and overlay them. Today, however, GIS goes beyond mere visual and qualitative correspondence; it allows us to test and quantify our assumptions about the past.

The structural approach in biogeography, as opposed to the floristic approach, is used here to describe vegetation and its implications for human settlement.[6] This classification of natural vegetation is conducive to the creation of regions because it de-emphasizes some floristic variability because of slight climatic or edaphic factors. For example, flatwoods occur to the east and west of the Mississippi alluvial valley between 30° and 31° north latitude. The major distinction between the two is the absence of shortleaf pine in flatwoods of southwestern Louisiana. This floristic difference is not sufficient to abandon their identical classification based on structural similarity.

At the most general structural level, the natural vegetation of Louisiana can be grouped into three broad categories: forest, prairie, and marsh. The forest category constitutes a forested landscape. Even a cursory examination of a map of potential natural vegetation reveals that forests predominate in Louisiana. This includes the shortleaf pine forests, longleaf pine forests, bottomland hardwoods (loblolly-oak), upland hardwoods (also called blufflands), flatwoods, gallery forests, and bottomlands (cottonwood, sycamore, and willow). The second broad category is that of prairie. The prairies of Louisiana are dry grasslands. They contain trees in concentration only along the margins of streams that flow through the area. The third broad category is that of marsh, which is classified as wet grassland. Louisiana's marshes are distinguished on the basis of salinity.

The distribution of potential natural vegetation types corresponds to a number of different physical conditions, one of the most noticeable of which is relief. By sorting the types on the basis of relief, we see that the bottomlands and cypress forests pretty well define the major low-lying alluvial valleys of the state. Marsh is limited to areas of coastal downwarping along the Gulf of Mexico. Prairies and flatwoods are located on lower terraces. The remaining forests are situated on the higher terraces and hills of the state.

The great wedge of the Mississippi alluvial valley makes it appear as if there are actually two regions of pine forests in Louisiana. The shortleaf pine, longleaf pine, and flatwoods (sometimes called longleaf pine flatwoods) of northern and western Louisiana and those of the Florida Parishes are actually part of a much greater pine belt stretching from East Texas through the Southeast to Virginia and the Carolinas.[7]

An additional distinction that can be made within the category of forest is between coniferous and deciduous forest. This does not mean that the forests are pure stands of either conifers (trees with cones and needle-like leaves) and deciduous (broadleaf trees that generally shed their leaves) species. Instead, it simply indicates that these species dominate numerically. This is frequently expressed as a percent of the total. For example, the shortleaf pine forest is defined as a forest with at least

50% shortleaf pine. The remainder of the shortleaf forest is composed of deciduous tree species such as various oaks and hickories.

A structural distinction of great importance to our understanding of the environmental zonation of species is that of upland versus lowland habitats. Some species within the above-mentioned coniferous group, for example, are upland species, while others are found in the lowlands. Almost all of the pines are upland species, as evidenced by their dominance in the hill and terrace regions of the state. The bald cypress, on the other hand, is a conifer that is found in the lowlands— alluvial floodplains, sloughs, and swamps.

Deciduous trees, often called hardwoods, also have a noticeable upland versus lowland distribution. Some hardwood forests are classified according to this upland-lowland dichotomy. The bottomlands forest is a lowland forest type in which hardwoods dominate; cottonwoods, sycamores, and willows are hardwood species that one frequently associates with the natural levee forest of alluvial valleys. Oaks and hickories comprise the most numerous deciduous species that make up the upland hardwoods, or blufflands, forest.

Two types of forest in Louisiana—bottomland hardwoods and gallery forests—have unique structural locations; they both are found along the margins of streams. The edaphic conditions along these streams permit the growth of hardwoods.[8] The bottomland hardwoods forest is characterized by a dominance of hardwood vegetation in an otherwise pine-dominated region. It is found in the shortleaf pine, longleaf pine, and flatwoods forests of northern and western Louisiana. The gallery forests, as the name implies, are forests of hardwoods that form a gallery, or arched covering, along either bank of streams flowing through the prairies of southwestern Louisiana.

The largest area of prairie, or dry grassland, is located in the southwestern portion of the state. There are several much smaller patches of grassland in the state, but the Southwest Louisiana prairie constitutes a true vegetation region. Interestingly, no satisfactory explanation for the existence of this large prairie region has emerged. A frequently cited suggestion is the presence of a hard clay-pan roughly a foot below the surface. The possibility of intentional periodic burning of vegetation by Native Americans to create clearings has also been suggested.

The existence of such an expanse of dry grassland in Southwest Louisiana is certainly an intriguing geographical problem, yet its genesis is not particularly crucial to this book.[9] There is no documentation to alter our assumption that the prairie existed in much the same configuration as presented here for the span of time under consideration.

Another grassland—the great coastal marsh of Louisiana—has some unique structural characteristics. According to Newton, the marsh, like the prairie, is also grassland, but because of continual saturation and varying degrees of salinity it is structurally and floristically different.[10]

> Still technically a grassland, the marsh was even called wet prairie during historic periods. It is, of course, completely an herbaceous cover, like the other prairies. The differentiation of the marsh lies principally upon the degree of saltiness of the water that keeps it continuously saturated. Of course, the amount of salt differs gradually and imperceptibly; even so, experts divide it into two, three, or four grades. Although the grades are arbitrary, they can commonly be described in terms of species tolerances.

The individual marsh types are merged into one category for the purpose of discussion in this book. The assumption is that except for pirates, runaway slaves, and hunters and trappers, the marsh was never host to human settlement.[11]

The Alluvial Landscape

Rivers created Louisiana. Some ancient rivers laid down the deposits that are now the uplifted hills of northern and western Louisiana. The succession of terraces, found mainly in southwestern Louisiana and the Florida Parishes, result from later alluvial action. Much of the coastal marsh is actually downwarping deltaic sediment. Finally, there is the present alluvial landscape.[12]

Rivers transported most of the sediment not only to modern-day Louisiana, but created the entire Gulf Coastal Plain. This material has been subject to modification by other physical processes since its deposition. Uplift and downwarping are the primary processes responsible for the creation of relief. There are significant areas of the state where old alluvial terraces are capped with loess soil, a deposit assumed to be aeolian in origin. Wind and wave action have produced elongated ridges—known as *cheniers*—that parallel the shoreline along the southwestern coast of the state.[13] Finally, another category of landform that is not attributable to alluvial processes is the salt dome. Salt domes are large masses of salt that have been thrust up from miles below ground through ancient and more recent alluvial sediments. The rivers of Louisiana remain, however, the foremost geomorphologic agents; this is especially true for the period of human occupation, or the past twelve thousand years.

The most impressive feature of the alluvial landscape of Louisiana is the celebrated Mississippi alluvial valley. This valley shows up vividly on any potential natural vegetation map as a wide zone of bottomlands and cypress forests. The Mississippi alluvial valley is bounded by Pleistocene terraces roughly fifty miles apart. These terraces form the valley walls. Most of the eastern valley wall between 31° and 33° north latitude is part of the State of Mississippi. And, for those who have gazed out across the Mississippi River from the vantage point of either Natchez or Vicksburg, the enormity of this physical feature is impressive indeed.

The southernmost extent of the alluvial valley is roughly formed by a line connecting the southwestern corner of the Florida Parishes and the southeastern edge of the prairies of Southwest Louisiana. From this line south, the river has made its way to the Gulf of Mexico creating a succession of deltas.[14] The most recent delta—the Balize—has been forming for the past millennium.[15]

Two other sizable alluvial valleys in Louisiana are the Red River Valley and, to a lesser extent, the Ouachita River Valley. These are also identifiable on any map of potential natural vegetation as fairly extensive zones of bottomlands and cypress forests. Unlike the Mississippi River in Louisiana, these rivers have many tributaries and rather extensive drainage basins.

Waterways in Louisiana go by various names, which can be the source of some confusion. This book follows locally accepted descriptive terminology when referring to a particular waterway, for example Tangipahoa "River," "Bayou" Teche, or Thompson "Creek." When referring to a stream in the abstract or in general the term "river" or "waterway" is used.

3. French Colonial Louisiana

The process of European exploration and colonization of Louisiana began long before anyone thought to build a city between the south shore of Lake Pontchartrain and the Mississippi River. During the first half of the sixteenth century, the Spanish, from their bases in the Caribbean, sent forth a number of expeditionary forces that encountered Louisiana's coast and interior, including, most notably, the "ill-fated" Narvaez expedition (1528) and the famed and equally disastrous De Soto *entrada* (1539-1543). These Spanish explorers and conquistadors rapidly lost interest in the area through their failure to locate mineral wealth, as they had in Middle and South America. Without the incentives that fortune provides, struggles with a resistant native population hardly seemed worth the effort.

The lower Mississippi Valley was virtually ignored by Europeans for more than a century following De Soto's death and his army's rout.[1] Spanish interests concentrated to the south and west. Other European powers, particularly England and France, cast a profit-minded eye toward the northeastern portion of North America, although successful colonization did not begin until the first decade of the seventeenth century.

The next European venture into the area for which we have documentation is that of Marquette and Joliet in 1673. They began their travels from the French settlements in the upper St. Lawrence

River, and, upon reaching the Mississippi, explored that river by canoe until reaching the mouth of the Arkansas. Actual penetration of the area that constitutes the present State of Louisiana came nine years later with the expedition of La Salle. He is credited with the "discovery" of the mouth of the Mississippi River and the proclamation of its valley as the possession of King Louis XIV of France.

Colonization of Louisiana is said to begin in 1699 with a party of Frenchmen and Canadians who first established a foothold on the northern shore of the Gulf of Mexico in the vicinity of Biloxi, Mississippi.[2] In charge of this group of about three hundred were the Le Moyne brothers—Pierre, Sieur de Iberville, and Jean Baptiste, Sieur de Bienville. From this base, which they called Fort Maurepas, they were able to reconnoiter their immediate surroundings, both physical and cultural. This included charting the lay of the land, particularly with respect to the great Mississippi River, and making contact with neighboring Indian tribes. Guillaume De L'Isle's map of Louisiana, published in 1734, serves as an excellent example of contemporary emphasis on the mapping of rivers and the location of Indian tribes.

The French continued to occupy sites along the Gulf Coast, later moving to Mobile Bay, Alabama, while increasing their knowledge of the lower Mississippi Valley through exploratory foray. The first permanent settlement within present-day Louisiana was not, as might be expected, on the Mississippi River, but was at Natchitoches well upstream on the Red River. This site was chosen as a clear challenge to the eastern periphery of Spain's dominion.[3]

In 1714, under the vigorous leadership of Louis Antoine Juchereau de St. Denis, a garrison for French troops—Fort St. Jean Baptiste— was established on the banks of the Cane River, an old course of the Red. Taking its name from the local Caddo Indian tribe, the town of Natchitoches grew up nearby. This little settlement, so far from Mobile, prospered. The cash crops of tobacco and indigo thrived in the fertile red soil of the floodplain. Cattle and horses multiplied; their increase having been attributed more to the rustling activities of Indians to the west than to the efficiency of French husbandry.

As if boldly thrusting chess pieces to the middle of the board, Spain countered by sending forth a contingent of troops from San Antonio and established the Presidio de Los Adaes a mere fourteen miles to the west of Fort St. Jean Baptiste. This posturing served to check the French "encroachment," but also tacitly confirmed La Salle's claim to all lands drained by the Mississippi and its tributaries.

Natchitoches grew in importance in subsequent years as an outpost on the western frontier. A symbiotic relationship developed between these two neighboring posts, far-flung from their respective administrative centers. In a time of jealously guarded trade restrictions, the Natchitoches area became, essentially, a great turnstile through which moved all manner of contraband. Instead of complying with regulations and requisitioning goods from Vera Cruz, more than a thousand miles to the south, the Spanish at Los Adaes and others along the *camino real* to the southwest found it easier and cheaper to get these goods from their French neighbors. In the other direction flowed cattle, horses, and mules.

Another site of early French settlement was at Natchez, Mississippi. Bienville was finally able to negotiate peaceful relations with the Natchez Indians in 1716 and built a fort—Fort Rosalie—on the bluffs overlooking the Mississippi River. This became a site of some importance for the French, although it ultimately spelled disaster for the Indians who gave the town its name.

In the early years of the French Colony, as in the English settlements along the Eastern Seaboard, Indians often kept the colonists from starvation. This is especially true of the French who settled among the Natchez. They acquired land that had already been cleared, concentrated on the cultivation of cash crops, and frequently purchased foodstuffs. Le Page du Pratz, who moved to Natchez in 1720, described this stratagem for survival.[4]

> I found upon the main road that leads from the chief village of the Natchez to the fort, about a hundred paces from the last, a cabin of the natives upon the road side, surrounded with a spot of cleared ground, the whole of which I bought by means of an interpreter. I made this purchase with the more pleasure, as I had upon the spot, wherewithal to lodge me and my people, with all my effects: the cleared ground was about six acres, which would form a garden and a plantation for tobacco, which was then the only commodity cultivated by the inhabitants. I had water convenient for my house, and all my land was very good.

Throughout the French colonial period the sequence of dependence, encroachment, and displacement characterized European-Native American relations. Nowhere is this more evident and vivid than in the Natchez area. The French in Canada generally were more successful in maintaining a rapport with the native inhabitants because they concentrated on developing trading partnerships and were less concerned with the appropriation of vast tracts of land.[5] St. Denis succeeded in the Natchitoches area by bringing the Caddo and other western tribes into his economic empire. The land-hungry plantation system, using African slave labor, left little room for native peoples who relied on the same arable land for their livelihood. This same scenario was played out in the English Virginia Colony a century earlier.

Although Natchitoches and Natchez were settled earlier, New Orleans gained prominence as the "primate city" of the colony. In 1717, French colonial leaders felt that the administrative center at Mobile was too far removed from the Mississippi River to be of strategic importance, so the site of New Orleans was selected. Settlers began erecting buildings the following year.

The site of New Orleans, as the locus of development for one of this country's major urban places, is indeed a puzzle.[6] How could a place so prone to flood, hurricane, and disease have been seriously considered for human habitation? How did it succeed in developing into a colonial and later territorial and state administrative and commercial center? One obvious answer is its location on one of the world's great rivers: the Mississippi. But the Mississippi River is 2,348 miles long; what did the early French colonizers find so attractive about that portion of the river that flows through a South Louisiana swamp?

Although some felt that higher ground along the river would be more desirable, such as is found above Bayou Manchac near Baton Rouge, the site of New Orleans prevailed. The presence of a small bayou— Bayou St. John—allowing navigation from New Orleans through Lake Pontchartrain to the Gulf was the answer. A contemporary account by engineer Le Blond de la Tour explains the attraction of this feature of the physical landscape.[7]

> In ascending the river, I have examined the most suitable sites for placing New Orleans and have not found a better situation than the spot where it is. The land is highest here and it is located at the portage of a bayou, a small river that flows into Lake Pontchartrain by which one can, at all times, communicate with New Biloxi, Mobile and the other posts more easily than by the lower river.

This seems to be the key as to why the site of New Orleans was selected. It was relatively close enough to the mouth of the river to be of strategic importance and it offered a "short cut" to the Gulf.

The site of early New Orleans was the natural levee along the left bank of the Mississippi River one hundred twenty miles from its outlet into the Gulf of Mexico. This natural levee is rarely over fifteen feet above sea level and slopes gradually away from the river. Areas of cypress swamp at or below sea level occur within a mile or two of habitable areas adjacent to the river.

In 1718, Bienville put fifty men to work clearing land and constructing some rude buildings. By 1719, a small clearing along the edge of the river boasted storehouses, barracks, and other residences. These buildings were placed in a haphazard manner. It was not until

1721 that the engineer de Pauger laid out a city plan.[8] This plan was based on principles of citadel fortification developed by Louis XIV's military engineer Vauban.[9]

New Orleans was laid out as a walled city in the European tradition, but only a handful of them were transplanted to North America.[10] The plan consisted of a central parade ground surrounded on three sides by administrative, military, and religious buildings. The blocks were laid out nine wide along the river and six deep. A higher artificial levee was built up fronting the river for nine hundred yards along either side of the settlement.[11] Most maps of the period show the city surrounded by ramparts and forts. The ramparts were earthen embankments topped with wooden posts. This plan is basically what survives today as New Orleans's famed French Quarter, or *Vieux Carre.*

After roughly two decades since the founding of New Orleans the Louisiana Colony was still in its infancy. As a proprietary colony of John Law's "Company of the West" and later the "Company of the Indies" (1717-1731), the settlers suffered continual setback and hardship. When the crown begrudgingly took back this liability known as Louisiana, matters failed to improve. Shipments of badly needed supplies were few and far between. And, the colony itself contained a fair number of indigents, exiled felons, and other unproductive inhabitants.

In 1731, the population of the colony was estimated to be seventy-five hundred. By 1744 this number had dwindled to roughly fifty-eight hundred, of whom approximately fourteen hundred lived in New Orleans.[12] Imported African slaves comprised a third of the total population of the colony at this time.

One saving grace from the standpoint of the peopling of the colony with productive settlers seems to have come from the large number of German peasants who immigrated to Louisiana during the 1720s and 1730s.[13] They settled primarily on both sides of the Mississippi River above New Orleans in St. Charles and St. John the Baptist parishes. The area became known as the German Coast, or *Côte des Allemands.* According to eminent Louisiana historian Edwin Davis, "these people had not come to Louisiana to make quick riches and return home or because they had been shipped out as criminals or moral lepers, they had come of their own volition to build homes and to make a new life for themselves and their families."[14] Their contribution to the survival of the colony comes largely from the abundance of foodstuffs from their gardens, which sustained both the idle and those concerned with cultivating of cash crops.

By 1740, occupation of Louisiana and the adjacent Gulf Coast was restricted to some highly specific areas. These included the coast between Biloxi and Mobile, adjacent to the Mississippi River from Natchez to just below New Orleans, Pointe Coupee Parish's False River settlement, along the Red River as far as Natchitoches, on the Upper Bayou Teche near Opelousas, and at an isolated post on the Ouachita River. Population distribution of the colony was already beginning to cluster in the capital, New Orleans, and along the Mississippi River for roughly fifty miles above and below this primate city.

The orientation of settlement toward Louisiana's major waterways reflected both a fundamental reliance on water transportation and the cultivation of the fertile alluvial bottomland, of which it is so abundantly endowed. A major impediment to expansion seems to have been a real or imagined hostility with the Indian inhabitants of the area.[15]

French Colonial Architecture

The architecture of the French colony of Louisiana in the year 1740 consisted of an assemblage of types popular to French Canada, as well as to the mother country.[16] Discounting the early temporary shelters that the French Canadians constructed on the Gulf Coast, most houses were either half-timber or log construction. The heavy half-timber houses of Louisiana and Canada have direct antecedents in Normandy, France, whereas log house construction was clearly the result of Canadian experience.[17] The architectural influence of the French Caribbean was just beginning to modify Louisiana structures in 1740.

41

Most houses of the first half of the French colonial period rested directly on the ground or had important structural members anchored in the ground. Common types such as *poteaux en terre*, or post-in-the-ground, and *planch debout en terre*, or upright-plank-in-the-ground, tended to rot fairly quickly in this humid semitropical environment. Drawings from the early eighteenth century show that the French were constructing these house forms that suited them well back in France or in Canada but were clearly not adaptive to Gulf Coast conditions.[18]

The French settlers of New Orleans, after about a decade of constant structural maintenance, modified their houses so that they rested on cypress posts.[19] These highly rot-resistant posts supported a sill upon which the same basic half-timber structure was built. This new design was referred to as *poteaux sur solle* (post-on-sill). The famed Creole raised cottage, where the house rests on raised piers or a full basement, is an architectural hallmark of the latter half of the eighteenth century.

An additional feature of the French half-timber, or *colombage*, construction was the placement of some sort of material between the mortised and tenoned heavy timber framework. This material was either brick or a mixture of mud and moss called *bousillage*. The habit of using bricks or mud mixed with some binding agent such as straw as nogging material was transferred from France, but the use of locally available Spanish moss was apparently adopted from local Native Americans. These filled spaces between the timbers not only strengthened the structure but also provided insulation against heat and cold.[20]

Because this nogging material would readily disintegrate if left exposed to the elements, the walls of the *colombage* house were covered with plaster or planks. The best method of exterior wall covering consisted of horizontal boards attached in clapboard-like fashion.[21] The wide galleries that later were incorporated into the framing served the additional function of protecting the walls.

The earliest roof form was a steep single-pitch, slightly hipped *pavilion* roof.[22] The roof and its underlying structure, in fact, are important classificatory elements in the evolution of Louisiana French architecture. The earliest form is a single-pitch roof with or without an optional gallery attached under its own framework and roof.[23] An intermediate form is a broken-pitch roof that incorporates a gallery. Finally, a single-pitch roof returns to popularity, but with the distinction that it now includes a fully engaged gallery. This classification is further subdivided according to additional structural innovations.

The single-pitch roof house, therefore, is the Norman and Canadian structure unmodified by West Indian influence. This was probably the dominant house form in Louisiana in 1740, although broken-pitch roof structures, which exemplified the Caribbean influence, had existed for some time on the Gulf Coast and were making an appearance in the Mississippi Valley.[24]

Another French building tradition that was contemporary with the initial single-pitch roof structure in Louisiana was the horizontal log, or *piece sur piece*, house. This distinctly French Canadian construction differed from the log house building tradition of the Upland South, discussed in Chapter 6, primarily in the attention to not only the notching element but finishing the entire log by planing it to make it square in cross-section.

The extent to which the French in Louisiana built in horizontal log is unknown. Some of the structures within the palisade of Fort Maurepas were probably of horizontal log construction, yet the structures within Fort St. Jean Baptiste were *poteaux en terre* and *colombage*.[25] An extant example of *piece sur piece* construction is preserved as the Pointe Coupee Parish Museum. It is an excellent specimen exhibiting the characteristic full dovetail notching and planed logs. Nevertheless, the relict cultural landscape and historical records suggest that the *colombage* house was considerably more widespread.[26]

The broken pitch roof structure with integral gallery is the quintessential French colonial house of the Mississippi Valley because it was built wherever French outposts occurred along the middle and lower Mississippi River.[27] To those unaccustomed to the vagaries of cultural diffusion, finding houses reminiscent of the French West

Indies in America's heartland (Missouri and Illinois, for example) may seem a little perplexing. Yet, there are extant French colonial structures practically in the shadow of the "Gateway to the West" arch in St. Louis, a monument to the "manifest destiny" of the American pioneer.

The Mississippi Valley French colonial house differed from French Caribbean structures in two important respects. First, the pitch of the inner roof of these broken-pitch roof structures resembled the *pavilion* roof.[28] The pitch of the West Indian French Creole house was considerably lower. Secondly, these houses were not raised above the ground to the same extent as the West Indian houses. The Mississippi Valley French colonial houses used the *poteaux sur solle* construction, which elevated the structure only slightly above the ground.[29]

The famous Creole raised cottage, the next significant architectural innovation to be distributed across the Louisiana landscape, was really more of a hallmark of the Spanish and British colonial period. One important component of this innovation was, as the name suggests, adopting the Caribbean trait of raising the structure well off the ground.

4. Spanish and British Colonial Louisiana

Some significant changes took place in the intervening years between 1740 and 1775. One profound transformation occurred in 1763 when France was forced to abandon its sovereignty over its possessions in continental North America: Canada and Louisiana. France's loss to the British in the French and Indian War resulted in the division of the Louisiana Colony between Spain and Britain. According to the terms of the Treaty of Paris, all territory east of the Mississippi River and north of Bayou Manchac, and following a line through pass Manchac through lakes Maurepas and Pontchartrain to the Gulf became British. Spain inherited that area west of the Mississippi River and south of the Manchac line. This included what has, since Iberville's day, been known as the "Isle of Orleans."

This change in political administration, in some respects, had little effect on the lives of the colonists who had settled under the French regime. French culture persisted vigorously under the umbrella of Spanish bureaucracy. Spain made little attempt to "Hispanicize" these Louisianians. French remained, for all practical purposes, the official language. The majority of Francophone residents, now under Spanish rule, felt betrayed by the French crown and abandoned, but continued to look toward Paris rather than Madrid for cultural identification and stimulation.[1]

The lands acquired by Britain, which became known as British West Florida, had been essentially devoid of a resident white population.[2] The one exception to this was Natchez, which later unfurled the Union Jack once the boundary separating Indian territory from British moved up to a line running eastward from the Yazoo at Vicksburg. Pensacola served as the capital of British West Florida and the Gulf Coast received the vast majority of new settlers during the 1760s.[3]

The British officer Philip Pittman made a reconnaissance of the Mississippi River and adjacent lands a few years after the Treaty of Paris and his noteworthy 1770 account bears testimony to the paucity of white settlers in what has become known as Louisiana's Florida Parishes.[4] Except for a short-lived post on the east bank of the Mississippi north of Bayou Manchac—Fort Bute—established by the British in 1765, the entire area seems to have been inhabited almost exclusively by various Indian groups.

The western portion of British West Florida, especially the lands along the Mississippi River, was rapidly and intensively settled during the decade of the 1770s. This coincided with the brewing of discontent and ultimate rebellion in the British Eastern Seaboard colonies. For all intents and purposes, this small portion of the Gulf Coast became an asylum for British loyalists.[5]

The non-Indian population along the Mississippi River portion of British West Florida is said to have increased from virtually nil in 1771 to roughly three thousand by mid-decade, of whom roughly one sixth were slaves.[6] A good number of these newly settled British subjects chose to reside in the Natchez area, but the Felicianas and Fort New Richmond—Baton Rouge—received a substantial influx as well.

One consequence of the French and Indian War that had considerable significance for the settlement history of Louisiana was the expulsion of the French living in Acadia, their heartland situated on the Nova Scotia side of the Bay of Fundy. This was the *Grand Derangement* popularized by Longfellow's epic poem *Evangeline*.[7] After being forced into exile by the British many Acadians looked toward the former French colony of Louisiana as a place to make their home.

The primary period of immigration of Acadians to Louisiana began in the 1760s. This punctuated stream of Acadian settlers resulted from their first having gone, after their expulsion from Nova Scotia, to other places such as New England, Maryland, the French Caribbean, and the mother country. Of the estimated eight to ten thousand exiles, it appears that roughly three thousand Acadians eventually made their way to Louisiana.[8]

The Spanish colonial administration in New Orleans, anxious to populate the colony, welcomed these Acadians with open arms provided they were willing to settle on the margins of the colony, hence extending the frontier. The first wave of immigrants was settled, according to strict Spanish instruction, on either side of the Mississippi River just upstream from the Germans. For this reason, the river portion of St. James and Ascension parishes has since been referred to as the Acadian Coast.

Modest grants of land fronting the river provided the *petite habitant* with resources that would sustain a modicum of self-sufficiency and comfort. The configuration of the grants conformed to the French arpent system whereby settlement along a waterway was maximized by laying out long narrow lots perpendicular to the river.[9] Grants given to Acadian families by the Spanish typically ranged from four to eight arpents of frontage by forty arpents in depth.[10]

The Acadians also settled down the Bayou Lafourche, along the Bayou Teche in the vicinity of the Post of Attakapas, or St. Martinville, and near Bayou Courtableau at the Post of Opelousas. The Opelousas area borders on the eastern margins of the great prairie region of Southwest Louisiana and the Acadians who settled here adopted a somewhat different lifestyle than their bayou brethren; they soon enthusiastically embraced the Spanish penchant for cattle ranching.[11] These Cajun cowboys realized that the prairies of Southwest Louisiana were ideal grazing lands, and they found a ready market for beef in New Orleans, as well as the plantations along the Mississippi River.

Settlement in Spanish colonial Louisiana in the year 1775 was densest in and around the capital, New Orleans. The plantations along the Mississippi River immediately above and below the city were the most developed and intensively cultivated. Another locus of population was along False River in Pointe Coupee Parish. This area, one of the earliest settled during the French colonial period, continued to prosper under Spanish dominion. A letter from Governor Alejandro O'Reilly to the Minister of the Indies in Madrid dated December 10, 1769 described the settlement density at Pointe Coupee.[12]

> The day after tomorrow, the 12th of the present month, I shall undertake my trip to Punta Cortada, which is situated up the river about fifty leagues from this city, and which, except the immediate surroundings of the Capital, is about the only well populated district in this province.

On the frontier of Spanish Louisiana of the early 1770s only four posts of any consequence existed. These were Attakapas, Opelousas, Natchitoches, and Rapides. One of the first orders of business of Governor O'Reilly was to commission Edwardo Nugent and Juan Kelly to make a reconnaissance of the area for strategic purposes and report on the population and condition of these posts. With respect to Attakapas and Opelousas, Nugent and Kelly's account is an excellent geographical observation and is quoted at length below.[13]

> Atacapas and Opelusas are two separate districts divided by a small Bayou which flows by Fusilier's [an individual with whom they lodged]. However, they can be considered as one, wholly alike in quality of land, products and live stock. These two districts extend 25 leagues in length and five in width, which is the inhabited part. The land has been cleared of trees where the houses have been built, which gives them the advantage of proximity to water and forest. The land between the estates consists of spacious prairies covered with admirable grazing of very high and slender grass which is free from thistle and thorn, etc. These prairies extend three and four leagues in circuit surrounded by clear forests through which small streams flow. Hence

the inhabitants maintain everything imaginable in the way of live stock, such as cows, horses, and sheep. There are excellent prairies covered with small grass suitable as pasture for sheep. There are also places where undoubtedly good crops of wheat could be raised if only ardor for its cultivation existed among the inhabitants. The products raised at present are rice, corn, and sweet potatoes as well as much live stock consisting of cows, heifers and some sheep. These products are used for the sustenance of the people and for trade with the native who ought to apply themselves to the raising of sheep and planting of corn, wheat, oats, rice, and flax since they have the most excellent land for these crops.

Their horses are good and they might raise a large number of them.

The inhabitants are not indolent and among them there are some industrious Acadians, who already have a good start towards an establishment which promises to be very useful in these lines of agriculture and cattle-raising. These people live in great tranquillity and accord, are law-abiding, and are well satisfied with the present administration and the kindness of the Government.

This account is fascinating not only for the description of land and life, but for the degree to which these observations are concentrated. The extent of settlement and its pattern, the present and potential agricultural production, and other aspects of the cultural geography of the region are all given in short order. Elements of what is to become an area of major Acadian settlement are present and await fruition. It is interesting to note how impressed these Spaniards were at the grazing potential of the prairies; doubtless their report reveals their cultural identity.

Nugent and Kelly's report, dated 1770, contains demographic information for the four posts visited. For the district of Attakapas, the census shows a total population of 199. The Opelousas district is listed as having a population of 312. Natchitoches, according to this report, consisted of about 80 houses and a fort, Fort St. Jean Baptiste.

The population of the district is given as 764. Their description of this important frontier outpost is also perceptive.[14]

> The perspective which Natchitoches presents consists of an almost circular portion of land with a diameter of about three leagues, crossed by the Red River, which divides itself into several arms, forming six small islands, on which the town and tillable land are situated [Cane River]. The whole vista is encircled by thick pine forests by which the view is limited on every side.
>
> The products of this country are mainly tobacco, corn, and rice.
>
> The live stock consists of cattle, a few pigs, and sheep, and a few domestic animals....There are several persons who are not farming and who do not have any honest way of living.

As in the description of Opelousas and Attakapas, the authors' ability to summarize the physical geography of the site and the cultural setting is excellent. It is evident also that some residents of this frontier town are engaged in some clandestine or illicit trade, an activity almost as early as the Louisiana Colony itself and one that would continue into the nineteenth century.

Rapides, modern Alexandria, is the last post mentioned in this incredible document. As this post had only recently been established and there was little to differentiate it from the surrounding wilderness, it received only cursory examination on the part of Governor O'Reilly's emissaries. The residents of Rapides, fifty-one in all, lived in eight rude houses and were just beginning to break ground for their tobacco plantations.[15]

As a summary of settlement in Louisiana circa 1775, the above-mentioned places formed the core areas. North and Southwest Louisiana were, and would remain for some time, devoid of a resident white population of any significance, with the possible exception of Fort Miro established on the Ouachita River a decade later.

The capital of the Spanish colony was not only the primate city, but the only city. Although the economic situation for New Orleans improved markedly during the Spanish period as the plantation economy of its hinterland boomed, the physical appearance changed little. In fact, according to accounts, there was some deterioration. Governor Unzaga wrote in 1775, "the fortress of this city is made of a stockade which forms six bastions that are almost destroyed by decay and the dampness of the soil. It is kept up only by continual repairs."[16] It is assumed that all structures were vulnerable to the process of decay of which Unzaga complained.

Disaster also contributed to inhibiting the growth of the city. Four years after the Governor penned the words quoted above a hurricane struck and destroyed much of the city. Fire would also plague New Orleans throughout the remainder of the century; especially devastating were the major conflagrations of 1788 and 1794. Nevertheless, Bienville's assessment of the advantageous situation of the "crescent city" was borne out during the Spanish colonial period. Despite its appearance, it remained the cultural, political, religious, and commercial center of the colony and region.

Population enumeration of the Spanish Colony completed in May of 1777 indicates that Louisiana had a total of 16,292 persons, half of whom were slaves, and the capital contained 3,206 residents.[17] The colony, therefore, had tripled in size since the 1744 census, and the capital had more than doubled. Evidently the plantation economy was expanding as well, if the number of slaves and their ratio relative to the white population are indicators. The number of slaves had more than quadrupled over the past thirty-three years and shifted from a third to a half of the total population.

Evolving Creole House Types

Despite the changes in house construction during the French colonial period, those early years of occupation appear to have been relatively stable architecturally when compared to the diversity displayed by Spanish and British colonial period houses. Just as the population remained predominantly French during this period, so too was the architecture. The Spanish and British made their contributions, certainly, but the greatest change came from the adoption and adaptation of the French West Indian house.

From the middle of the French colonial period until the Treaty of Paris more and more French Creole houses were constructed fully raised in the West Indian style. In fact, this distinctive vernacular house type was commonplace along the Mississippi all the way up to the French settlement of St. Louis in what is now the American heartland.[18] When used to describe buildings, the term "creole" connotes a New World hybrid of Old World forms. It is linked particularly with the Caribbean, which seems to have been the zone of mixing and innovation beginning in the sixteenth century.

A type of Creole house that became especially popular in New Orleans was one that had a brick ground floor, or basement, and second floor, which was really the main living area, constructed in the *colombage* fashion.[19] Although probably dating to after the devastating 1788 New Orleans fire, a house in the French Quarter that embodies all of the structural attributes of this once popular type is "Madame John's Legacy" on Dumaine Street (Figure 3).[20]

Figure 3. Madame John's Legacy, New Orleans. Photograph by the author.

In the latter half of the eighteenth century the Mississippi Valley French colonial house gave way in popularity to a house with a fully engaged gallery under a single-pitch roof. Because the gallery was often a "wrap-around gallery," the single-pitch hipped roof appeared like an umbrella over the house proper.[21] An excellent example of this emerging style is "Homeplace," constructed circa 1790 in St. Charles Parish (Figure 4).

Figure 4. "Homeplace," St. Charles Parish. Photograph by the author.

The large raised Creole plantation house is perhaps the most vivid rural example of French architecture of colonial Louisiana according to modern popular conception. Its popularity has extended into the modern subdivision where architects have designed some of their nicer homes in "the Louisiana style," aping the exterior appearance of these large French plantation homes. Nevertheless, as mentioned earlier, the latter half of the eighteenth century was a period of incredible diversity with respect to the French Creole house, and plantation homes such as "Homeplace," although beautiful, represent only one form among many.

One area where this architectural diversity took place was in the floor plan of the house. The interior arrangement of rooms, attached rooms, and gallery configuration offered a seemingly limitless potential combination of plans.[22] There is also an evolutionary sequence to these various floor plans. Suffice it to say that in general the possibilities for variation and complexity became greater as the French Creole house evolved.

Some of the floor plan variation seems to be explained by the influence of the Georgian architectural style then popular in the British Eastern Seaboard colonies.[23] French Creole houses beginning in the mid-eighteenth century became more symmetrical in plan. Later examples even adopted the central hall. This movement in architectural design toward greater structural symmetry reflected a much wider stylistic trend.

The simple gable roof with the gable end to the side was another architectural change that added to the diversity of the later smaller French Creole house (Figure 5). This roof form came into common usage in the 1750s and 1760s, especially in the vicinity of New Orleans. As Edwards explained, the newly arrived Acadians displayed a clear preference for this gable roof house.[24]

> Acadian (French Canadian) settlers began to arrive in New Orleans from Haiti in 1765, a decade after they had been cruelly deported en masse from Nova Scotia. They adopted as their own a gabled-roof cottage with a built-in porch—a diminutive, single-room form of the Creole house then popular in the New Orleans area and familiar to them from Haiti.... Beginning in the 1790s, a module with two rooms of equal width and two doors on the façade became the standard in many areas settled by the Acadians.

Figure 5. Smaller French Creole Houses. Acadian Village, Lafayette Parish. Photograph by the author.

A considerable amount of descriptive literature on the smaller Creole, or Acadian, cottage exists, but scholars continue to discuss the origin, diffusion, and architectural detail of this popular house type.[25] For example, Edwards notes that the basic form experienced further architectural transformation with the placement of a loft stairway and the addition of a "false gallery" once it took root in Louisiana.[26]

The Acadian Upper Teche house is another folk type in the French tradition, but its distribution is limited. It is essentially a smaller Creole house without the integrated gallery, and it is not raised. Because it does not display the Caribbean traits of the other Creole houses, some students of Louisiana's architectural history argue that it alone qualifies as a true "Acadian" house.[27]

British Creole houses were also built during the latter half of the eighteenth century in the blufflands between Baton Rouge and Natchez. These structures were mainly Lowland South (Tidewater) plantation houses that were modified by the Caribbean architectural influence.

Even though the British Creole house resembled the French Creole house in some fundamental respects, such as half-timber construction atop a full basement, engaged galleries, and a non-symmetrical floor plan, upon closer inspection telltale features distinguish between the two.[28] A British Creole house has a somewhat different floor plan, a slightly broken-pitch roof, and external chimneys on the gable ends. One British Creole house in West Feliciana Parish, "Oakley" (ca. 1790), is sometimes mistakenly cited as an example of the French Creole raised cottage type because of shared Caribbean traits that the structure exhibits.

To summarize, the Spanish and British colonial period of the late eighteenth century was characterized architecturally by considerable Caribbean influence and subsequent modification. These modifications tended to create a number of competing forms, most subject to change through time. This was the era of the Creole cottage, whether urban or rural, large or small, French or British. It was the period that Edwards has termed, "the wonderful florescence of the Creole tradition."[29]

5. Territorial Louisiana: Between Colony and Statehood

Several significant changes occurred in Louisiana in the intervening years between 1775 and 1810. One dramatic event, brewing in the British colonies in the East, was the American Revolution. Louisianians in the Spanish colony joined the cause under the leadership of Governor Bernardo de Galvez and captured the British fort at Baton Rouge on September 21, 1779. They moved on to capture Mobile and Pensacola, and the surrender of British West Florida officially took place on May 10, 1781. The whole of Louisiana now belonged to the King of Spain.

Following the War for Independence, Americans began their great westward migration. Into the valleys west of the Appalachians came a steady stream of land-hungry pioneers. Typical of the times is the life of William Darby, a highly motivated and talented individual.[1] At age six Darby accompanied his parents across the Alleghenies in 1781. He grew up on the frontier and acquired a taste for new lands and the opportunities that they offered. In 1799, at the age of twenty-four, he went to seek his fortune, and like so many before and after him, he floated down the Ohio and Mississippi rivers and disembarked in Natchez. There he met his wife who moved with him in 1805 to Opelousas. He became a capable surveyor and an important figure in the history of Louisiana cartography.

Any map of Louisiana colonial land claims with a composite of French, Spanish, and British cadastral survey confirmed by the United States Congress displays the settled portions of the state that William Darby and his contemporaries would have known. Interestingly, settlement areas on such a map are easily identified even without benefit of physical features other than the Mississippi River. Colonial settlement shows up clearly along waterways such as the Red, Teche, Vermilion, Lafourche, Bogue Chitto, and Mississippi. It is also significant to notice where colonial land claims are scarce or absent. The Atchafalaya Basin and coastal marsh are conspicuous as areas essentially devoid of land claims. And, as will become evident in the next chapter, appreciable settlement had not yet been established in the vast northern and western portions of the state.

With the massive influx of settlers into the region between the Appalachians and the Mississippi, Americans began to view the Spanish colony of Louisiana as crucial to their national interests. Given the difficulty of overland communication between east and west, the Mississippi River system became an expedient outlet for a growing number of Americans. Spain, however, controlled the outlet of the Mississippi, and, as a consequence, a sizeable portion of the United States as it then existed had to rely on a "foreign" city to get products to market.

The attention of the young nation of the United States focused on Louisiana at the close of the eighteenth century. Spain was protective of its port and eyed the burgeoning American traffic with suspicion. A 1795 treaty with Spain allowed Americans the right to export goods out of New Orleans, but in 1802 this privilege, so necessary to western Americans, was denied.[2]

Louisiana was but a pawn being moved about in the larger game of European geopolitics. As a concession to Napoleon Bonaparte, the new leader of France who was beginning to flex his muscles on the continent, Spain retroceded its Louisiana colony by the Treaty of San Ildefonso on October 1, 1800. Sentiments among most Americans ran high, and even President Jefferson referred to the nation that possessed New Orleans as "our natural and habitual enemy."[3]

While France moved slowly to reinstate its administration in Louisiana, American negotiators in Paris moved swiftly to impress upon Napoleon the importance of the lower Mississippi River to the American people. The initial intention of Robert Livingston and James Monroe was to bargain for the Isle of Orleans and the right to navigation on the lower Mississippi. To everyone's surprise, however, Napoleon, who was beginning to view the whole of Louisiana as a liability, offered to sell the entire colony to the United States. The famous Louisiana Purchase agreement, which was signed on April 30, 1803, ranks alongside our acquisition of Alaska from Russia as one of the most significant bargains in American history.

The purchase was indeed a bargain. America paid about four cents an acre for an enormous piece of real estate, over eight hundred thousand square miles. Davis puts the Louisiana Purchase into geographical perspective.[4]

> The purchase of Louisiana almost doubled the land area of the United States. The territory was more than thirteen times larger than New England, nearly three times larger than the thirteen original states of the Union, and roughly a third of the continental area of the present-day nation.

The economic impact was felt almost immediately. The tonnage of cargo shipped out of New Orleans jumped almost 50% the following year.[5] This sudden prosperity also opened the floodgates to a surge of eager settlers. Americans were on the move; the destination for many was the old Louisiana colony itself.

Not all of old Louisiana had been given over to the French in 1800 and subsequently transferred to the United States in 1803. Spain retained West Florida. It held on to the "Florida Parishes" until September 23, 1810 when a contingent of armed planters stormed the Spanish fort in Baton Rouge and proclaimed the area as the independent Republic of West Florida.[6] This tiny republic was short-lived, however, because less than three months later the governor of the Territory of Orleans, William C.C. Claiborne, annexed it. Congress officially joined the Florida Parishes—that zone between the Pearl and Mississippi rivers— to the Territory of Orleans on April 14, 1812.[7]

The Territory of Orleans itself was separated from the vast lands included in the Louisiana Purchase by Act of Congress on March 26, 1804.[8] This new territory included all land drained by the Mississippi River south of the 33rd parallel. That same year, the newly created legislative council divided their territory into twelve counties. Three years later, division of the territory into nineteen parishes began to erode the power of the county system of administration. According to Davis, these counties were, "apparently retained for the purpose of electing representatives and levying taxes, and gradually the functions went out of existence."[9] Kyser explained that the brief tenure of the county system of civil administration was the result of, "resistance of the Latin inhabitants of Louisiana to the new order."[10] He further stated that, "well-known dislike for the new judicial system was undoubtedly one of the strongest factors working against the preservation of the counties as originally created."[11] At any rate, in Louisiana the term "parish" has lost its ecclesiastical meaning and has become synonymous with the civil division of county, which is used in the rest of the United States.

The western boundary of the new Territory of Orleans was something of a problem. Since the time of St. Denis this area had been a zone of contention and the solution to this boundary problem between the United States and Spain was the informal creation of what has become known as the "Neutral Ground." The most contested land lay between the Sabine River to the west and the Arroyo Hondo and Calcasieu River to the east. According to Davis, "this no-man's land was filled with lawless squatters who robbed and killed until 1810, when a joint expedition of Spanish and Americans drove them out."[12] A large portion of South Louisiana was also of questionable ownership. The western boundary of the present-day State of Louisiana was not fixed until the Adams-Onis Treaty of 1819.

The 1810 federal census of the Territory of Orleans included twenty parishes and excluded the Florida Parishes. All but three parishes in the territory had populations numbering fewer than five thousand individuals. The total population of the territory was 76,554, a third of whom resided in Orleans Parish. New Orleans, the only metropolis in the territory, had a population of 17,242, and was, according to the 1810 census, the largest city west of the Appalachians and the fifth largest city in the United States. This growth had its effect on the old colonial city. With the expansion of New Orleans in the three possible directions complete by 1810, city officials decided to remove the old fortifications and physically connect the suburbs with the city. The wide boulevards that bound the French Quarter today—Canal Street, Rampart Street, and Esplanade Avenue—are the physical remnants of the old walled city. A similar landscape can be seen in ancient European cities once fortified for protection.[13]

Just as the population of Orleans Parish was concentrated in New Orleans, so too the populations of St. Landry and St. Martin parishes were mainly in the vicinity of Opelousas and St. Martinville (Attakapas). Most of southwestern Louisiana, however, remained sparsely populated. North Louisiana in 1810, on the other hand, was essentially vacant. The huge parishes of Natchitoches and Ouachita had a combined population of only 3,947, with most living in the vicinity of the town of Natchitoches along the Cane River or along the Ouachita River in or near Fort Miro, later Monroe. An attempt had been made later in the eighteenth century to encourage settlement in the Ouachita region, but this ended in failure. In 1795, the Spanish granted a huge tract of land amounting to twelve leagues square, or about six hundred fifty thousand acres, to the Baron de Bastrop. He, in return, agreed to settle this grant with five hundred families. When he succeeded in enticing only a tenth of that number to settle in the region his grant was revoked.[14]

American and Haitian Influence

The first shock waves of American migration to Louisiana were felt in the city of New Orleans. Immediately following the Louisiana Purchase the city filled with Americans who brought with them, among other things, their own customs of architectural propriety and style. One of the most famous architects of the early Classical Revival, Benjamin Henry Latrobe, was working in New Orleans in these early years and saw the proverbial handwriting on the wall: "I have no doubt but that the American style will ultimately be that of the whole city."[15]

Actually, the French Creoles dug in their heels and their *Vieux Carre* remained relatively free from this American onslaught. The wide boulevard of Canal Street became the boundary—the original "neutral zone," as the grass strip between opposing lanes of traffic is known—as the unwelcome Americans built their own city upstream. Even still, a few Federal style and early Classical Revival style buildings were constructed in the French Quarter, the work of father and son architects Benjamin Henry Latrobe and Henry S. Latrobe.

One of the first non-Creole structures was the new Custom House, designed in 1807, which was built in the Federal style out of red brick from Philadelphia.[16] The New Orleans Custom House is a building that would not have been out of place in Philadelphia, Baltimore, or especially the growing city of Washington; cities that were rapidly growing during the Federal Period (1780-1820). In the *Vieux Carre*, however, this public structure and a few brick residences with slate roofs were considered architectural oddities.[17]

American architectural influence was strongest, naturally, in the growing American sector, the so-called Faubourg St. Mary. Although Lewis described this area as, "now half ghetto half skid row" because the affluent and middle-class American residential neighborhoods moved progressively farther upstream along the crescent of the Mississippi natural levee, it was once the site of numerous structures in the "American style."[18]

The architectural style that Americans introduced to Louisiana in the period around 1810 is the Federal style. This style is characterized by a low-pitched hip or gable roof, dentil molding under the eaves, smooth façade, semi-circular or elliptical fan light above a paneled front door and perhaps with Palladian windows.[19] The favored building material for a Federal style structure was wood frame in New England and brick in the Middle Atlantic and the South. The Federal style was quickly replaced by the Greek Revival style around 1820.

In New Orleans, some structures were built in this style a little later than its period of national popularity. The Hermann-Grima house (1831) in the French Quarter, for example, is relatively late for a Federal house. It is, nevertheless, "one of the best examples of American influence on New Orleans architecture."[20]

Another group that migrated to New Orleans in large numbers following the Louisiana Purchase was composed of French Creole planters and their slaves, as well as free blacks, also known as "free persons of color." They came mainly from Haiti, driven out by slave insurrections that were sweeping the West Indies.[21] In 1809 alone, an estimated six thousand people moved from that former French Caribbean country to New Orleans.[22] In terms of the effect of this immigration on the cultural landscape, it seems that one of the most enigmatic of Louisiana's house types—the shotgun—was introduced by Haitians who came to New Orleans at this time.

Although fully cognizant of the competing explanations for the genesis of the shotgun house, Vlach asserted that, "the origins of the shotgun are not to be found in the swamps and bayous of Louisiana but in Haiti."[23] Actually, this is not the first time someone suggested that Haitians brought the shotgun house to Louisiana; geographer Fred Kniffen did so in 1963.[24] At any rate, Vlach's research is the most thorough and comprehensive to date and merits serious consideration.

In the Notarial Archives of New Orleans are drawings of shotgun houses from the early nineteenth century. These drawings advertised houses that were for sale, and it appears that the oldest rendering of the shotgun type was a house in the French Quarter that was sold in November of 1833.[25] This date is considered a *terminus ante quem*, or firm date before which the house was actually constructed. The association of Haitian free blacks in New Orleans either employed in the building trade or contracted for a typical Haitian shotgun—a *maison basse*—to be built has also been established. As you can imagine, in the wake of the Louisiana Purchase New Orleans was experiencing a significant housing shortage, and recently arrived Haitian immigrants and doubtless many others chose to build the precursor of what we know today as the shotgun house.[26]

The unique feature of the shotgun tradition is the gable front orientation (Figure 6). The shotgun house is one room wide and three or more rooms deep. Additions at the back of the structure can give the shotgun an "L" or "T" plan. Earlier forms are usually vertical board construction. The roof can be gable or hipped, and if there is a porch it can be fully or partially integrated with the roof, or simply attached as in a shed porch. The chimney, if present, can be located in a variety of positions, but not at the gable ends.

Figure 6. Shotgun Houses, Baton Rouge. Photograph by the author.

In its most basic and unadorned form the shotgun house type has a strong association with the plantation system. Outside of New Orleans the shotgun functioned as quarters on plantations throughout the South. The slave quarters portion of a plantation frequently amounted to a row or double row of shotgun houses, and was a key architectural component of the plantation settlement pattern.

From the earliest urban examples in New Orleans and rural examples on sugar and cotton plantations to relatively recent times, the shotgun house has been predominantly an African-American dwelling. Some shotgun houses in New Orleans, however, have undergone "gentrification" and are no longer occupied by poor blacks.

6. The Upland South Comes to Louisiana

The election of Andrew Jackson in 1828 as seventh President of the United States resoundingly proclaimed a dramatic shift in national politics and society. To be sure, "Old Hickory" was a hero of the battle of New Orleans and had attracted national attention. Nevertheless, the new president differed from his predecessors in two important respects: he was raised in a familial and social setting that was far from affluent and he was a product of, and spokesman for, the new West. All previous presidents of the United States emerged from well-to-do families. Their interests were decidedly those of the Eastern Seaboard states. Jackson was a new breed. His parents were poor immigrants from Ireland, not landed gentry. He was raised on the frontier of the Carolina uplands and Tennessee, not in any of the old culture hearths of colonial America. Although he was indeed an exemplary individual, he was something of a symbol of thousands of individuals of lesser notoriety.

Andrew Jackson was perhaps the personification of the new breed of American settler coming to Louisiana by 1830. This new breed has been termed the "Upland South Culture."[1] The Upland South Culture congealed in the southern Appalachians between 1725 and 1775, and then spread in a westerly and southerly direction for roughly the next seventy-five years. This group's capacity to push the frontier forward has been attributed to a body of culture traits that was "preadapted" to conditions encountered in the Southeast woodlands.[2]

In general, the Upland Southerner sought out an environment similar in its physical geography to that of "home."[3] The characteristics of climate, soils, hydrology, topography, and vegetation were scrutinized as to how closely they resembled those of the environment of their upbringing. This keen interest in finding a like environmental setting was not so much for nostalgic reasons (although that may have been a factor), but for the practical reasons of making a living. Historian Frank Owsley explains: "The farmer who seeks a country similar in appearance, climate, and soil to the old community in which he has lived makes the basic and sound assumption that he can continue in the new country to grow the field crops, fruits, and vegetables, the tillage, habits, and marketing of which are part of his mental furniture."[4] This underscores the importance of cultural preadaption.

By 1830, a sizable number of individuals from the Upland South core area in the southern Appalachians had made their way to Louisiana. This influx of new settlers was composed of individuals who varied in their degree of sedentism but shared culture traits known collectively as the Upland South Culture.

Although the westward and southwestward movement of Upland South people has been characterized as consisting of "waves" of people with differing strategies for survival, the sequential nature of this occupation has been called into question. The traditional interpretation holds that the vanguard of the Upland South Culture was the hunter-herder. These individuals moved into the hill regions of the state that heretofore had only seen Native American occupation. The hunter-herder pursued a subsistence-settlement pattern that can best be described as nomadic. They stayed in an area for as long as the game and the forage remained available. Their agricultural activities were limited to small plots of corn and vegetables.

According to this view, the hunter-herders were followed by the "plain folk" agriculturists. This group, like the hunter-herder, took full advantage of unsurveyed public domain land and moved about at will. They were considerably more settled than the hunter-herder, but still, by all accounts, their shifting cultivation and free-ranging cattle and hogs constituted an extensive land use. The huge, virtually unoccupied expanse of piney woods in Louisiana proved to be an ideal habitat for this culture group.

Frequently, however, the hunter-herders were not supplanted by the agriculturists; they became them. They simply began to supplement their income through crop production until that became a primary economic pursuit. The two "waves" of Upland South occupation of the piney woods, therefore, actually represent two adaptations to the same environment whose sequence is probably illusory. The primary distinction seems to be the degree to which agriculture was involved. At any rate, the Upland Southerner was spatially, if not culturally, distinct from those involved in the prosperous plantation regions of the lowlands and blufflands.

Frank Owsley, in his book *Plain Folk of the Old South*, convincingly makes the point that these Upland Southerners deliberately selected the uplands and piney woods, rather than being forced out of the more fertile river valleys by wealthy planters. Owsley satirically reiterates the view that the plain folk were social outcasts relegated to life beyond the pale in the piney woods.[5]

> They had been pushed off by the planters into the pine barrens and sterile sand hills and mountains. Here as squatters upon abandoned lands and government tracts they dwelt in squalid log huts and kept alive by hunting and fishing and by growing patches of corn, sweet potatoes, collards, and pumpkins in the small "deadenings" or clearings they had made in the all-engulfing wilderness. They were illiterate, shiftless, irresponsible, frequently vicious, and nearly always addicted to the use of "rot gut" whiskey and to dirt eating. Many, perhaps nearly all, according to later writers, had malaria, hookworm, and pellagra. Between the Great Unwashed and the slaveholders there was a chasm that could not be bridged.

Rather than making a distinction based on moral fiber or degree of literacy, a contrast between the Upland South and the wealthy planter class is really one of ethnicity and culture. The Upland Southerners were predominately Scotch-Irish and German. The planters of 1830 were either French or English Creoles.

Of course many French Louisianians had been involved in plantation agriculture since the early days of the colony, but the English were later arrivals. Many planters of English extract relocated to the alluvial lands and blufflands of Louisiana in the 1770s to avoid the inevitable rebellion that was in full ferment, as well as to take advantage of an environment well suited to a variety of cash crops. These English planters are known as the Lowland Southerners because of their origin in the tidewater lowlands of the Eastern Seaboard. Newton concluded that when considering the South as a culture region, "the most striking cultural fact to emerge is the overriding distinction between the Upland and Lowland (Tidewater) South, between the frontier-Appalachian small-holder and the coastal Cavalier planter."[6]

The terms Upland South and Lowland South imply both a cultural and geographical distinction. Not only was there a difference in ethnicity between the "plain folk" and the wealthy planter, but this condition had a geographic expression that replicated itself in Louisiana. The Scotch-Irish and Germans settled in the piedmont and mountains of the southern Appalachians, while the English dominated the coastal plain. In Louisiana, this topographical separation was still maintained, albeit to a lesser degree.

For many Upland Southerners, Louisiana was not their final destination. Those who came to the Florida Parishes were more likely to remain, but many who entered Louisiana through Vicksburg or Natchez were actually on their way to Texas. These were the Americans who wrested the "Republic of Texas" from Mexico in 1836.

The main overland route traveled by Upland Southerners bound for Louisiana and Texas was the Natchez Trace. If they chose to push on toward Texas, on foot or by horse, the linkage with the *camino real* leading to Nacogdoches, San Antonio, and locations farther into Mexico, was the town of Natchitoches, Louisiana.[7] Connecting Natchez to Natchitoches was a road resembling a "V" with Alexandria at its apex. This road skirted Catahoula Lake, crossed the Red at Alexandria, and traversed the west banks of the Red and Cane rivers to Natchitoches. Two other routes of lesser importance that led to Texas were the Vicksburg-Monroe-Natchitoches route and a route that went from Opelousas to Lake Charles.

The growing interest in the western portion of Louisiana, which was also the southwestern corner of the United States, is evidenced by not only known routes but by the establishment of forts as well.[8] In 1822, the United States Army felt the need to fortify the "neutral ground" along the Sabine River, so, under the direction of Colonel Zachary Taylor, Fort Jessup was constructed along the *camino real* west of Natchitoches.[9] To the south and also somewhat inland from the Sabine River boundary, Fort Atkinson was built in 1830 in the vicinity of Lake Charles.

Another related signal of the mass migration of the Upland Southerners at this time was the sale of lands belonging to the Caddo Indians in Northwest Louisiana. This amounted to a huge portion of the state because the Caddo's homeland extended from the Sabine River, the modern state boundary with Texas, to the Ouachita River in northeast Louisiana.[10] In 1835, the United States government persuaded the Caddo to sell this land for $80,000.[11] Although some scholars have argued that the sale of Indian land initiated rapid American settlement of North Louisiana, it appears that the preemption of this property by Upland Southerners had been going on for some time. In a manner of speaking, then, it was not the treaty that resulted in rapid settlement of the region, but vice versa.

By 1828, the giant northwest Louisiana parish of Natchitoches had a sufficient number of people in its northern portion that a separate parish—Claiborne—was formed. This population is attributable to the influx of Upland South settlers rather than planters establishing profitable cotton plantations up the Red River. The latter would have to wait another decade until a huge logjam, known as the "Great Raft," was cleared out and the Red River above Natchitoches made navigable.

Other portions of the state experienced population growth that equaled or exceeded that of North Louisiana, but the initial occupation of this vast area stands out in bold relief when one looks at the settlement of the state around the year 1830.[12] This was indeed a time characterized by a group of people whose adaptation to the land differed markedly from that of the majority of settlers who had arrived in Louisiana since 1699.

North Louisiana in the 1830s was the fastest growing area of the state. Comparing the 1810 population of the parishes of Natchitoches, Ouachita, and Catahoula with that of 1830 for roughly the same area, which now included the newly created Claiborne Parish, it can be seen that the population increased by three and a half times: from 5,111 to 17,390. The population of Ouachita Parish increased by almost five times. By way of contrast, the Mississippi River parishes from Ascension Parish to the Gulf, those roughly sixty miles above and below the "crescent city," doubled in population from 1810 to 1830. This area includes the old Acadian Coast, the German Coast, and the thriving city of New Orleans. The population of the whole area increased from 39,576 to 88,113.

Clearly, the population of those Mississippi River parishes increased a great deal more in terms of raw numbers, but expressed as a rate of growth North Louisiana can be said to have been growing more rapidly. The lower river parishes contained much that was conducive to population growth, both by natural increase and immigration. This area was the famous "sugar bowl," where the production of sugarcane was heavily dependent on slave labor. The number of slaves in this area, in fact, actually tripled from 1810 to 1830, whereas population as a whole doubled. Nevertheless, by assessing population growth and expansion in terms of rates of increase and the occupation of heretofore "vacant" terrain, the Upland South settlement of North Louisiana merits notice.

The other significant part of the state that received settlers from the Upland South was the Florida Parishes. Unfortunately, as mentioned earlier, these parishes were Spanish at the time of the United States 1810 decennial census. Therefore, it is not possible to make any statements about population growth. The blufflands of the Felicianas and East Baton Rouge Parish constituted an area that people from the Lowland South found attractive. The piney woods of the three eastern parishes—St. Helena, Washington, and St. Tammany—attracted Upland South settlers, and were thus more akin to neighboring counties in Mississippi to the north and east, as well as the piney woods parishes of North Louisiana.

The difference in the intensity of settlement between the western and eastern Florida Parishes is apparent. Even though the eastern three parishes made up about two thirds of the total area, it contained only about one third of the population. Much of St. Helena Parish was initially settled by Upland Southerners in the first two decades of the nineteenth century.[13] Washington and St. Tammany parishes both had sparse populations in 1830; the heaviest concentrations being along the north shore of Lake Pontchartrain and along the Tangipahoa, Pearl, and Bogue Chitto rivers.

The Upland South Building Tradition

The Upland South settlers differed from their French neighbors in many cultural respects, and the kinds of houses that they built and lived in was one of them. One distinction is the importance of log construction to the Upland South building tradition.[14] It was not a common construction technique among the French of South Louisiana, although there is evidence to suggest that *piece sur piece* structures were built to some extent.[15]

Log construction in the Upland South building tradition continued in some parts of Louisiana until around 1880. Where sawn lumber was available and people had the desire to do so, Upland South types were built of frame construction covered with clapboard. Generally speaking, although some Upland South houses were framed using half-timber construction, the technique known as balloon framing rapidly replaced log construction after the Civil War.

Another aspect of the Upland South building tradition is the use of the British "pen" or "bay." The Upland South building tradition is a subset of the pen tradition, which is shared with two other Anglo-American culture regions: the Middle Atlantic and New England.[16] The single-pen house is the fundamental building block of the pen tradition. All other pen tradition houses are made up of a combination of these single-pen structures. Some double-pen, saddle-bag, or dog-trot houses started out as single-pen structures.

The single-pen usually measures between sixteen and twenty-five feet in front and between sixteen and twenty-one feet on the side.[17] Construction material was generally of horizontal logs, but later lumber was used. The chimney was exterior and attached to the gable end. If there was a porch, it was either attached or under a broken-pitch roof.

The double-pen house is, as the name suggests, two single-pens put together under the same gable roof. The dimensions are usually around sixteen by thirty-two or sixteen by thirty-six feet. They generally have chimneys located at both gable ends. A front porch is frequently attached or under a broken-pitch roof. A shed addition, and sometimes an ell, may have been attached to the back of the house. The double-pen house was used as plantation quarters up and down the Mississippi and Red rivers, although it was by no means as common as the shotgun in that regard. It is found across the Upland South, but is not a frequent form in Louisiana.

The saddle-bag house is essentially a double-pen with a central chimney. If it has a continuous-pitch roof it may be mistaken for a small Creole house. Upon closer inspection, however, architectural features such as door placement, room division of the rear shed, and the use of *bousillage*, usually reveal the house as either Upland South or Creole.[18]

The dog-trot house (Figure 7) is made up of two pens separated by an open passageway under a gable roof.[19] The open area between the two pens—the "dog-trot"—may be likened to a central hall, which led geographer Milton Newton to refer to the dog-trot as "frontier Georgian."[20] Some frame dog-trot houses, in fact, have enclosed the dog-trot and constructed a central entrance, thus making it difficult to distinguish it from a central hall house.

Figure 7. Dog-Trot House. LSU Rural Life Museum, Baton Rouge. Photograph by the author.

The dog-trot house in Louisiana was constructed of many different building materials, but log and lumber predominate. Chimneys are usually at the gable ends and outside. Full-length porches, also known as galleries, are found on the front and back, a function of being located under the broad gable roof. Dog-trots were placed on wooden, stone, or brick piers which raise them off the ground from one to three feet.

The bluffland house is a distinct type of unknown age and with limited distribution. As the name suggests, this type is most commonly found in the bluffland area of the Florida Parishes and in adjacent counties of Mississippi. It consists of a story and a half structure with a wide central hall, and seems to have been a variety of the dog-trot house. Like bookends, chimneys flank the gable ends of the bluffland house. There is usually an ell. One hallmark of this type is the "false gallery" extending out beyond the engaged porch or gallery. This false gallery, which may be original to the initial house construction or added at some later date, wraps partially around the side as well.[21]

The Upland South building tradition, therefore, is a collection of genetically related types. As folk housing is wont to do, general forms remain relatively constant despite changes in construction techniques and material. Many of these houses span the entire nineteenth century essentially unchanged. By 1830, these types, with the possible exception of the bluffland house, were beginning to dominate large segments of the cultural landscape of Louisiana. These Upland South house types as a rule lacked architectural style. Aside from Newton's "frontier Georgian" explanation for the bilateral symmetry evident in Upland South structures, there is little in the way of nationally recognized architectural style that can be attributed to them.

7. The Golden Age of the Plantation

In 1850, the greatest concentration of millionaires in this country was along the Mississippi River between Natchez and New Orleans. This opulence resulted from the plantation system of agriculture. The combination of fertile alluvial or upland loess soils, suitable climate, efficient river transportation, slave labor, and a world demand for the cash crops of sugar and cotton resulted in a landscape that is, in many respects, consistent with today's popular conception of the antebellum South. To be sure, the plantation system at mid-century in Louisiana was a fact of life for most people, whether planter or slave, New Orleans merchant, Acadian *petite habitant*, or piney woods squatter. The planter class controlled the economy and the political scene. They provided role models for others to emulate, and they owned outright a significant percentage of the black population of the state. It would not be hyperbole, therefore, to state that the plantation system was the single most important feature of the cultural geography for a Louisiana of the 1850s.

A plantation, by definition, is a large landholding, usually more than five hundred acres, that concentrates on the production of a single cash crop. Louisiana plantations would usually produce moderate amounts of a variety of other things, frequently staples, but clearly their goals did not include self-sufficiency. As a result, a hinterland of farms that supplied these needs developed hand-in-hand with the plantation economy and prospered along with it.

Prior to 1850 a number of cash crops had their period of popularity; among these were indigo, rice, and tobacco. Sugarcane and cotton came to dominate the plantation scene in Louisiana, but tended to concentrate in different regions of the state. The so-called "Sugar Bowl" developed in the Mississippi alluvial valley south of the thirty-first parallel, with an extension up the Red River to include Rapides Parish.[1] Cotton was produced over much of North Louisiana, but a very noticeable cotton-producing region, the "Tensas Cotton Belt," developed from the Felicianas northward along the Mississippi alluvial valley and adjacent uplands.[2]

Obviously, an important ingredient in any agricultural endeavor is the crucial and basic medium for plant growth: soil. Agriculturists since the early French colonial era had recognized the richness of the alluvial bottomland environment. The fertility of these alluvial soils is due to the accumulation of regular over-bank flooding resulting in incredibly deep deposits capable of sustained yield. By 1850, in fact, a portion of the Mississippi alluvial valley had been cultivated for more than a century without noticeable reduction in crop yield.

The uplands, or blufflands, whose deep and fertile loess soil was known to be agriculturally productive since the earliest days of French settlement (Fort Rosalie in Natchez). As part of the Old Natchez District from the British colonial period, the Felicianas, which have some of the deepest loess in the state, remained a landscape characterized by Lowland South plantations. Significantly, West Feliciana Parish produced more cotton per square mile than any other place in Louisiana, and most of the South for that matter.[3]

The climatic requirements, or tolerances, for the two significant plantation crops—sugarcane and cotton—are different. The most important difference is that sugarcane is a more tropical crop and its distribution is limited to South Louisiana. Cotton, on the other hand, is not restricted, being able to thrive from the warm moist coast to the cooler drier interior. A relatively dry season in late summer and fall, however, facilitates the cotton harvest. Both crops are vulnerable to a climatic event not uncommon in Louisiana: the hurricane

One of the most important factors in the location of antebellum plantation agriculture was efficient river transportation, specifically the advent of the steamboat.[4] Other forms of watercraft had moved goods and people up and down the navigable waterways of the state since prehistoric times, but cargo capacity was limited and travel against the current was always difficult.

Plantations produce a bulk commodity, and, as is true with the economic geography of any bulk commodity, transportation costs are a vital ingredient in the equation that determines profit. For plantations of the 1850s this translated into a sort of imaginary line inland from all navigable rivers frequented by steamboats. This line separated the zone of profitability, based on relative ease of transportation, from the zone of where profit rapidly diminished with distance.

The steamboat was really the only option in 1850 for the planter who needed to get crops from field to factor, usually an agent in New Orleans. Railroad construction was in its infancy in 1850, and the roads of the period were generally in a deplorable and unreliable state. With respect to the latter, Taylor notes that, "antebellum roads in Louisiana were so poor as hardly to deserve the name, and that situation did not improve until the twentieth century."[5]

The steamboat had actually been a fixture in the realm of transportation in Louisiana since the first one came down the Mississippi to New Orleans in 1812. Technical innovations of a shallow-draft hull and more powerful steam engines increased the steamboat's ability to travel against strong current and ply shallow bayous and rivers at low stage.

The steamboat opened up North Louisiana, so to speak, where steamboat and settlement became almost synonymous terms. The people of Fort Miro, a settlement on the west bank of the Ouachita River, were so impressed by the arrival of the first steamboat in 1819—

the *James Monroe*—that they decided to rename their town Monroe to commemorate such a momentous event.[6] This prepared the way for their participation in the cotton boom.

Another important North Louisiana town's name is intimately associated with the steamboat: Shreveport. After clearing the "great raft" on the Red River above Natchitoches in the 1830s, Captain Henry M. Shreve and some associates founded the town of Shreveport in 1838. From its very inception, Shreveport was the major port for the shipment of cotton out of Northwest Louisiana.

For much of North Louisiana, then, the steamboat not only facilitated but also made possible the expansion of plantation agriculture. Towns like Monroe and Shreveport owed their growing importance to the steamboat, and plantations began to line the waterways of the northern part of the state much as they had expanded on the Mississippi above and below New Orleans a century earlier. Kniffen and Hilliard emphasize the symbiotic relationship between steamboat and settlement: "By midcentury, every stream, if navigable only at high water stage, had steamboats pushing into it to bring in supplies and carry out cotton."[7]

A component of plantation agriculture of the antebellum South was slavery. The production of sugarcane and cotton were both labor-intensive activities that relied almost exclusively on the labor of black slaves. The habit of using black African slaves was as old as the colony itself. For example, a shipload carrying five hundred slaves arrived in 1719 just as New Orleans was being built.[8] By 1850, half of the population of the State of Louisiana was black and most of them were slaves.

Although the importation of African slaves became more difficult, particularly because of the intervention of the British beginning in 1810, it continued in an increasingly clandestine manner. Within the United States, sentiment had polarized the country. Despite arguments on moral grounds, it remained a fact that Louisiana's economy, its *genre de vivre*, depended on cotton and sugarcane, which, in turn, were dependant, according to the methods of production of the time, on slave labor.

The association of slaves and plantations clearly correlates with the alluvial valleys of the Mississippi and Red. The only exceptions to this pattern seem to be Rapides, Lafourche, Jefferson, and Orleans parishes. They can be explained by more Upland Southerners living in the piney woods of Rapides relative to the slave population, more Cajuns along Bayou Lafourche relative to slave population, and the urban dwellers of the New Orleans area in Jefferson and Orleans parishes relative to slaves. Also, East Baton Rouge Parish and the Felicianas technically belong to the uplands, or blufflands, environmental classification, but their association with the plantation region of the state has already been noted. It is also interesting to examine the other areas of the state where slaves comprised less than half of the parish population. These areas coincide with the piney woods of the eastern Florida Parishes and North Louisiana, as well as the prairie region of Southwest Louisiana.

The population of the state in 1850 shows a growth pattern that, in part, can be attributed to the expansion of the plantation system. One of the most noticeable aspects of population growth can be seen in the change in the number of parishes in North Louisiana from 1830 to 1850 and the population growth, particularly in the "Tensas Cotton Belt."[9]

Between 1830 and 1850, sixteen new parishes were created, of which thirteen were in North Louisiana. The area covered by the seven North Louisiana parishes in 1830—Avoyelles, Catahoula, Claiborne, Concordia, Natchitoches, Ouachita, and Rapides—was divided into 20 parishes. This area north of the thirty-first parallel had increased at an even more accelerated rate than the interval between 1810 and 1830. In 1830, the population of these parishes totaled 33,111, but twenty years later the same area contained a population of 151,757, an increase of more than four and a half times the 1830 figure.

During the same period, the so-called "Tensas Cotton Belt" experienced a population increase of five and a half times the 1830 figure. In 1830, the population of the elongated parish of Concordia, which contained most of North Louisiana's share of the Mississippi alluvial valley, had a population of only 4,662. By 1850, the same area had split into three parishes—Madison, Tensas, and Concordia—with a combined population of 25,571.[10]

To further place the cotton boom of North Louisiana into statewide perspective, Orleans Parish increased from 49,826 in 1830 to 119,460 in 1850. This is an increase of 2.39 times. Expressed differently, Orleans Parish, which means essentially the primate city of New Orleans, had roughly seventy thousand more residents. The growing towns and countryside of North Louisiana had roughly one hundred twenty thousand more residents. Of course, it is somewhat unfair to compare the population of a single city to a huge area covering half of the state, but the point here is that the tide of population increase was no longer greatest in the south. North Louisiana by 1850 was becoming a real entity in terms of population.

The city of New Orleans, however, was not only the fastest growing city in the South, but it was changing in the composition of its population as well. Its sinuous urban development upstream along the natural levee had been the trajectory of expansion since the Louisiana Purchase, and in 1850 actually comprised three cities in one. There was the American sector, or "Garden District," the historic French core, and an area that came to be dominated by recent Irish and German immigrants. Historian Roger Shugg points out: "Of these three sections the American was wealthiest, the French most populous, and the Irish-German poorest in both numbers and money."[11]

Another observation that should be noted when comparing the 1830 population distribution to that of 1850 is the pattern of population distribution that is revealed with the creation of Calcasieu Parish from the massive parent 1830 parish of St. Landry. It can readily be seen that the majority of population had resided in the eastern half of the area. In fact, this is the old Opelousas area that had been a popular settlement area since the late eighteenth century. Once the area is divided in half the census figures reveal this fact vividly; Calcasieu has only 3,914 residents to St. Landry's 22,253 people. In terms of settlement, then, it appears that the southwestern portion of the state, along with Sabine Parish and three of the four easternmost Florida Parishes, can be characterized as only sparsely populated.

In sum, Louisiana in 1850 can be fairly described as "the Golden Age of the Plantation." Cotton and steamboats came to dominate the cultural landscape of North Louisiana and the western Florida Parishes. In the case of the former, it was responsible for a great deal of initial occupation of the area, and in the latter it simply intensified an existing Lowland South plantation economy. Sugarcane, of course, continued to be the plantation crop of choice for South Louisiana. New Orleans solidified its role as entrepôt for this agrarian culture despite the growth of towns up the Mississippi, Red, and Ouachita rivers. Almost everything continued to pass through this world-class port, and population growth reflects these flush times. It was, however, the culmination of a system about to collapse.

Antebellum Plantation Architecture

It is fitting to discuss the domestic architecture of plantations circa the year 1850 because most of the "great" plantation houses of Louisiana were built within two decades prior of the Civil War. This is the period of the quintessential Greek Revival style plantation home such as "Oak Alley" (1836), "Houmas House" (1840), and "Madewood" (1848). It is the period in which nationally popular architectural styles come into their own in Louisiana, sometimes with incredible idiosyncratic results. The styles that are the hallmark of antebellum plantation architecture are Greek Revival, and, to a lesser extent, Gothic Revival and Italianate.

The domestic architecture of plantations also consists of some recognized types. These types include two types of Upland South plantation homes, as well as the Lowland South plantation type. The temporal affiliation of these types is, of course, much greater than the years surrounding 1850.

Two Upland South plantation house types that are part of the pen tradition are the hill plantation I-house and the Carolina I-house. The hill plantation I-house is sort of a box two rooms wide, one room deep, and two stories high. Both stories have a central hall and a porch running the full length of the front of the house. Chimneys are generally exterior and at both gable ends. In some respects, it resembles a two-story dog-trot structure.[12] The Carolina I-house is similar to the hill plantation I-house except for the full-length one-story porch in front and the one-story shed across the back. Found throughout the Upland South, this type had its origin in the western Carolinas. In Louisiana, the Carolina I-house occurs most frequently in the western Florida Parishes.

The Upland South plantation house differs from other Upland South types in degree rather than kind. The common building block—the pen tradition—can be clearly identified in the construction of these houses. Where and how they differ from Upland South types seems to be the obvious association with plantation agriculture. Where Upland Southerners engaged in plantation agriculture the hill plantation I-house and the Carolina I-house were frequently built. This is undoubtedly the case in the western Felicianas, where plantation houses such as "Oakley" (1810) bear the unmistakable stamp of the Carolinas.[13]

The Lowland South plantation house, like the hill plantation I-house, is a box form two rooms wide and two stories high, but two rooms deep. It differs in some other respects also. The chimneys, for example, are generally interior. The Lowland South plantation house tends to have a hipped roof and elements of Georgian architectural style typical of the Tidewater South. Also in keeping with its Tidewater heritage, a favored construction material was brick. "Madewood," for example, used an estimated sixty thousand slave-made bricks in its construction.[14]

The quintessential Lowland South plantation house is "Nottoway" (1859), and no better example exists for the demonstration of Lowland South migration to Louisiana (Figure 8). The house was built by John Hampden Randolph of Virginia, who named his plantation home after his native county back in the Old Dominion State. Although its size—it is the largest plantation home in the South—and its Italianate architectural style attract immediate attention, its Lowland South box-like core is readily apparent.

Figure 8. "Nottoway." Iberville Parish. Photograph by the author.

Of the house types just mentioned, architectural style in the period around 1850 was an important feature only in the Lowland South plantation house. These houses always displayed architectural style of one sort of another, whereas Upland South types seldom did. In later years these other types took on stylistic attributes, either structural or decorative. For the late antebellum period, however, the plantation house of lore was the Lowland South type in Greek Revival, Gothic Revival, or Italianate style.

The Greek Revival style began its period of popularity in America in the Northeastern United States around 1820. Although American interest in the classical world of ancient Greece and Rome can be traced to the "enlightened" ideas that inspired the American Revolution and was later expressed in Federal and Jeffersonian (Roman Revival) architecture, a clear "Hellenophilia" began to sweep the country beginning in 1820. The Greek Revival style amounts to the architectural component of a wider cultural revival that was sparked by the Greek struggle for independence. The diffusion of this Romantic Movement can be seen in North American place-names, where classical town names such as Athens, Rome, Sparta, and Syracuse spread across the country from 1820 to 1860.[15]

The most common Greek Revival stylistic features are columns and pilasters, moldings, pedimented gables, heavy cornices, and horizontal transoms (Figure 9).[16] In terms of form, the front-gable house is another feature of the Greek Revival style. Architects later used the front-gable orientation for designs in different styles. Although there developed numerous attributes and regional variations, the common conception of the Greek Revival style as white, gable-fronted and columned "temples" is not too far off the mark.

Figure 9. "Stanton Hall," Natchez, Mississippi. Photograph by the author.

Given its period of popularity at the time when the plantation economy of Louisiana was booming and when many planters were engaged in an architectural "one-upsmanship," it is not surprising that they chose to build in the most fashionable style on a massive scale. And the Greek Revival style was certainly an appropriate medium for Herculean architecture: the taller the columns and the higher the ceiling, the better.

A plethora of columns, however, should not be interpreted as ostentatious display given the syncretic nature of South Louisiana architecture. Many of Louisiana's Greek Revival plantation homes seem to be surrounded by these large columns which support a wide hip roof. This actually represents an adoption of the wrap-around gallery of the French Caribbean plantation home. Architects designing Louisiana plantation homes in the Greek Revival style apparently took into consideration some of the environmentally adapted characteristics of the Creole raised cottage. Examples of the "full colonnaded" variety of the Greek Revival plantation house include "Oak Alley," mentioned earlier, and the majestic "Dunleith" (1856) in Natchez, Mississippi.

A somewhat later architectural style, the Gothic Revival, was nationally popular from about 1840 to 1880. However, it was never as popular as the competing Greek Revival or Italianate styles. In addition, from the standpoint of regional receptivity, the style was not nearly as well received in the South as it was in the North. Most examples in Louisiana are antebellum.

The Gothic Revival style is characterized by a steeply pitched gable roof, gables with decorative vergeboards, and pointed-arch shaped windows among other features.[17] Lumber was the usual building material of domestic structures, although stone and masonry were also used. Understandably, it was a common architectural style for churches.[18] Larger stone and masonry examples frequently have towers and castellated parapets, and resemble medieval castles out of a Sir Walter Scott novel.

One of these "castles" is the Old Louisiana State Capitol (1850), situated on the banks of the Mississippi at Baton Rouge. Designed by the noted New Orleans architect James H. Dakin, it is a spectacular example of the Gothic Revival style.[19] Its imposing towers and parapets, however, failed to impress one outspoken and experienced traveler of the Mississippi River—Samuel L. Clemens.[20]

> Sir Walter Scott is probably responsible for the Capitol building; for it is not conceivable that this little sham castle would ever have been built if he had not run the people mad, a couple of generations ago, with his medieval romances....It is pathetic enough that a whitewashed castle with turrets and things...should ever have been built in this otherwise honorable place; but it is much more pathetic to see this architectural falsehood undergoing restoration and perpetuation in our day, when it would have been so easy to let dynamite finish what a charitable fire began, and then devote this restoration money to the building of something genuine.

It is evident that Mark Twain was not taken by the Gothic Revival style!

Some plantation homes, and even associated outbuildings such as carriage houses and outhouses, were built in the Gothic Revival style. "Afton Villa" (1849) in West Feliciana Parish is probably the finest example of a Gothic Revival plantation home in Louisiana. "Orange Grove" (1850) in Plaquemines Parish was also constructed in the style. And, although the incredibly ornate plantation home "San Francisco" (1853) has been described as belonging to the "Steamboat Gothic" style, implying that it is a variety of the Gothic Revival, it is actually more Italianate (Figure 10). The term "Steamboat Gothic" derives from a 1952 novel of the same name by Frances Parkinson Keyes.[21]

**Figure 10. "San Francisco," St. John the Baptist Parish. Photograph by
the author.**

The Italianate style was roughly contemporaneous with the Gothic
Revival. Its period of national popularity began in 1840 and continued
until 1885. Some important features of this style include a low pitched
roof with wide eaves frequently accompanied by decorative brackets, tall
narrow round-headed windows with hood molding, ornate entrance,
and a square tower or cupola.

The Italianate style in Louisiana had a wider application than the
Gothic Revival. The most notable examples of plantation homes built
in the Italianate style in Louisiana are "Nottoway" and "San Francisco"
mentioned earlier. But, besides its use as an architectural style for
plantation homes, it appears in other building forms as well; stores,
banks, city halls, business blocks, and churches were all built in the
Italianate style. Its greater flexibility in design offered wider application,
hence its greater popularity.

An architectural influence that had minor plantation home
manifestation has been grouped under the rubric "Exotic Revivals."

In the lower Mississippi valley the plantation home that best fits this category is unquestionably "Longwood" (1860) in Natchez, Mississippi. It is something of a hybrid structure; the shape is octagonal, an extremely rare form with a brief period of national popularity (1850-1870). The decorative treatment is Italianate, and the onion dome atop the huge cupola is Exotic (Oriental) Revival.

From the standpoint of architectural style, therefore, Louisiana structures built around 1850, particularly plantation homes, were not just diluted imitations of architectural forms found in the Northeastern United States. Although the nationally popular Greek Revival, Gothic Revival, and Italianate styles found initial expression in the North, the plantation region of the lower Mississippi valley had its share. Clearly, some of its inhabitants participated in wider cultural movements that included an architectural component, and they did so with incredible results. The Greek Revival architecture of Louisiana, for example, is some of the best this country has to offer.

8. The Civil War and Reconstruction

In the minds of many, the change that occurred in Louisiana between 1850 and 1870 is undoubtedly one of the most dramatic in American history. A society whose members were not held in bondage enjoyed prosperity, optimism, and cultural vigor that was unequaled until halfway into the twentieth century. As a consequence, those who have concerned themselves with the writing of this nation's history have devoted more ink to the interval of these two decades than any period before or since. One eminent historian of Louisiana described the period as "the most tragic in all Louisiana history."[1] It was, of course, the American Civil War, 1861-1865, as well as its causes and aftermath.

It is beyond the scope of this book to give an accounting of what, in some quarters, is referred to as the "War for Southern Independence."[2] Others may assess a value judgment of what was undeniably a cultural cataclysm. The fact remains that the American South in general and Louisiana in particular were, in 1870, engaged in a reconstruction.[3] This reconstruction did not amount to a replication of the social, political, and economic order that existed prior to the Civil War. Instead, it was actually a restructuring of a culture.

Looming large was "the peculiar institution" of black slavery. According to historian Joe Taylor, this was the key issue that precipitated the Civil War: "Despite the obfuscation of speeches on states' rights and other over-fervent nationalistic rhetoric, Louisiana and the South seceded from the Union primarily because secession was felt to be necessary to preserve Negro slavery."[4] One of the most celebrated effects of the War was the emancipation of slaves, an event that was ruinous to the plantation economy of the South. Many a plantation in Louisiana atrophied because the labor upon which its actual existence relied was no longer available. This fact was noted by many, including the capable geographer Samuel H. Lockett. Travelling through Terrebonne Parish in 1869, he observed that "many of the once splendid plantations...were utterly abandoned. The residences, Negro quarters, and sugar houses were going into decay."[5]

During the same reconnaissance of the state, Lockett had the opportunity to visit the newly established farmsteads of former slaves and had favorable impressions of their husbandry. One individual, Pierre Noir, was "reputed to be worth ten or twelve thousand dollars in hard cash, in addition to the large herds of horses, cows, and sheep he owns, and the fine farm he so successfully cultivates."[6]

To be sure, not every plantation in Louisiana disappeared and not all emancipated slaves were as successful as was Pierre Noir. Cotton plantations fared better than sugar plantations during Reconstruction because of the relatively high post-war demand for cotton and that sugar production required a substantially greater capital investment in machinery. The sugar plantations that did survive adopted the wage system, while sharecropping, or tenant farming, became the usual mode of production on the cotton plantation. The end result for the majority of blacks who remained with the plantation system as wage laborers or sharecroppers was that their quality of life was probably not greatly improved.

After emancipation, the options open to most blacks in rural Louisiana were to remain in plantation agriculture as wage laborers or sharecroppers, to establish farmsteads of their own, to move to New Orleans, or to leave the state altogether. Just like the white yeoman farmers who chose sharecropping, blacks frequently discovered that this arrangement resulted in a sort of debt-peonage similar in many respects to the condition of slavery. Many found themselves hopelessly indebted to the plantation store, from which they had purchased basic necessities on credit, usually at greatly inflated prices, and were forbidden to move off the plantation until this debt was cleared. Nevertheless, for a significant percentage of blacks this presented the most viable alternative.

The establishment of a subsistence farmstead by blacks was another adaptation to conditions after the Civil War. Quite often these farmsteads were clustered into settlements, such as the Darlings Creek settlements of St. Helena Parish.[7] These subsistence farmsteads occurred outside of the prime plantation areas, mainly in the piney woods.

Black-flight off the plantations and into New Orleans began during the early years of the Civil War. It has been estimated that perhaps as many as ten thousand slaves streamed into New Orleans after the Union army, commanded by Major General Benjamin F. Butler, secured South Louisiana in 1862.[8] They were encouraged to return to the plantations as freedmen, but many decided to stay and eke out a living in the stagnant economy of wartime New Orleans.

Some freedmen decided to emigrate from the state that had enslaved them. Nearly three thousand black families moved to Texas, and later in the decade many blacks got "Kansas Fever" and decided to try their hand at becoming wheat farmers in Kansas.[9] For various reasons, most returned. Actually, a black exodus from Louisiana on any appreciable scale would not occur until industrial jobs in the North beckoned in the twentieth century.

White yeoman farmers as a group, were as negatively impacted by the Civil War and Reconstruction as anyone. First of all, Louisiana's enlisted Confederate soldiers came mainly from the ranks of the "plain folk." They enthusiastically joined the cause and constituted a great share of the sixty-five thousand men mustered to fight the Yankee.[10] Thousands never returned to their piney woods farms. Those who did return often found them desolate and devoid of livestock; their families merely trying to cling to the land as best they could.

Another casualty of the War that caused profound distress to planters and farmers was the tremendous loss of livestock. According to Newton, "horses, mules, and oxen were in that time, after all, the basic underpinning of agriculture and industry. To lose half of these beasts…literally crippled production."[11] These animals were in short supply for years to come.

Upland Southerners continued to pour into North Louisiana as settlers or as transients bound for Texas, but times were difficult. Despite the fact that free homesteads in the public domain amounting to a quarter section of land, or one hundred sixty acres, were available throughout the 1870s, many simply found a piece of land to their liking and settled without any form of legal title. Land was the only thing during Reconstruction not in short supply. Enjoying some of life's luxuries was out of the question, and some could not even afford necessities. For the yeoman farmer accustomed to a certain amount of hardship and privation the only solution was to simply keep working.

The destruction of property during the War in Louisiana was greatest along most of the length of the Mississippi alluvial valley above New Orleans, along the lower Red River alluvial valley, inland between Alexandria and Opelousas, and down the bayous Teche and Lafourche. Damage coincided with the theaters of battle, as well as with the richest plantation areas of the state capable of sustaining armies. So, not only were the plantations located here deprived of their slaves and livestock, there was often little left but the land itself.

The plantation generally survived, but frequently under different ownership. Many antebellum planters, particularly sugar planters, were ruined and had no alternative but to sell. The irony of this change in ownership is that not only did the plantation system survive, there was actually an increase in the number of plantations after the War.[12] The increase in large land-holdings has been attributed to sharecropping, or tenant farming, because the profit received from the tenants sometimes exceeded that received from the crop. Although cotton sharecropping ended, for all intents and purposes, in the 1950s, the trend toward absentee plantation ownership and land consolidation has continued to the present.

The effects of Reconstruction are reflected in population figures and the distribution of population. First of all, in the twenty-year interval between 1848 and 1868 only one new parish—Winn—had been created. This is in marked contrast to the parish growth spurt of the 1830s and 1840s when sixteen new parishes were created. This is, of course, the result of approximating the more-or-less idealized parish size and that North Louisiana could not be expected to fission parishes indefinitely. However, it also seems to be a simple function of population growth.

The state's population was rising steadily according to the decennial census until the decade of the Civil War and Reconstruction. In 1840 the population of Louisiana was 352,411, in 1850 it was 517,762, on the eve of the Civil War (1860) it was 708,002, then in 1870 it had grown less than twenty thousand.[13] The population gain in the decade between 1860 and 1870 was only one tenth that of the decade leading up to 1860. The loss of eleven thousand Confederate soldiers only partially accounts for this drop in a rising population trajectory. The indirect loss of the potential progeny of those who died, both soldier and civilian, as a result of the War and its deprivations to the rate of natural increase is yet another factor. However, the most significant causes of this demographic change are declining immigration and increasing emigration.

In 1870, Louisiana's population was beginning to grow again, and was expanding into new areas. Cities other than the primate city of New Orleans were in the incipient stage of urbanization. Twelve Louisiana cities had a population over one thousand.[14] Clearly however, the Crescent City was, in terms of the 1870 population, the only city worthy of the name. The great disparity between New Orleans and even the next largest city, Baton Rouge, illustrates this distinction. Even though Baton Rouge had been the state capital from 1846 until 1862, New Orleans still had both population and power. In fact, New

Orleans was nearly eight times larger than all these other eleven cities combined. Roughly one quarter of the state's population resided in New Orleans, whereas only 3.4% resided in the other above-mentioned cities. It remains, however, that the state in 1870 can be characterized as roughly 70% rural and 30% urban.

Two other areas of economic growth were beginning to appear in 1870: railroads and lumber. Both are hallmarks of the next chapter focusing on 1890 because they had brought about important changes in the settlement pattern of the state. So, as the old plantation system with its attendant reliance on steamboat transportation was beginning to fade from view, the railroad and lumber boom came into sharper focus.

The Nadir of Building in Louisiana

Although Natchez, Mississippi had been separate politically from Louisiana since the 1795 Treaty of Madrid, culturally it was as tied to the plantation system and the lower Mississippi River as any place in Louisiana. Many who lived on those Pleistocene bluffs overlooking the Mississippi River actually operated plantations across the river in Louisiana, and had close ties with the down-river ports of Baton Rouge and New Orleans. It is valid, therefore, to illustrate the impact of the Civil War and Reconstruction by examining this once important city that figured prominently in the history of Louisiana since the days of Iberville and Bienville.

Natchez, like much of Louisiana, lay devastated in 1870. Physically, the city remained, but its antebellum vibrancy, which was a tribute to the now defunct plantation system, was gone. Twenty years earlier Natchez had been one of the most important cities in the United States. The Civil War succeeded in halting its rampant prosperity as surely as Mount Vesuvius put a stop to Pompeii. As the New Orleans author Harnett T. Kane put it, "all that Natchez had left was its past....In these drowsing years, when few newcomers came and few old people left except on that last ride to the cemetery, Natchez lived in and with and, some observed, for its past."[15]

Natchez is noted for having one of the greatest concentrations of antebellum plantation architecture in the South for the simple reason that the economy remained so depressed that little new was built and the old was not subject to remodeling. For the historical geographer, it is one of this country's most inspiring relict landscapes, both under the hill and above. Much of the city and many of the surrounding plantation homes have been restored over the past half-century to the splendor of lore circa 1850.

Few places in Louisiana were as "frozen in time" as was Natchez as a result of the Civil War and Reconstruction. Many lesser places eventually expired or revived economically. This, of course, had its architectural implications of structural decay or restoration, modification, and addition. For the period of 1870, however, with the possible exception of New Orleans, the rest of Louisiana resembled Natchez.

One curious folk house type makes its appearance during Reconstruction: the "camel-back" house. The camel-back house is a member of the shotgun tradition whose distribution is mainly limited to New Orleans, and to some extent, Baton Rouge. The camel-back is an innovative adaptation to the urban environment. It is apparently a shotgun with its addition not on the side or rear, like its rural counterpart, but on top of the back portion of the house.

Architectural historian Samuel Wilson confirms the speculation that the camel-back grew out of the Reconstruction as a form of inexpensive housing to accommodate tenants in the urban environment of New Orleans.[16]

> The most significant addition to the Vieux Carre scene...
> was the proliferation of narrow frame cottages of the
> "shotgun" variety, mostly doubles, with the occasional
> "camel back" where the rear portion of the house was
> made two stories. Houses of this type were erected in
> all parts of New Orleans in the 1870's, 1880's, and 90's

> wherever land could be bought at a low price and cheap
> houses could be built for rental purposes.

According to geographer Pierce Lewis, the origin of this unusual house form, "is uncertain, but may have resulted from tax laws which assessed the value of a house according to its height along the streetfront."[17] Whatever the causes for the origin of this peculiar house type, the camel-back is a strictly urban type, found predominately in New Orleans, whose period of popularity appears to begin around 1870 and lasts through the rest of the nineteenth century.

It is in keeping with the general impoverishment of the state in 1870 that the house type to emerge from the ashes of the Civil War was a hybrid of the shotgun, a type frequently associated with slave quarters in antebellum times. Houses based on the shotgun form, in fact, were probably popular house types in both urban and rural settings during Reconstruction because they were inexpensive and simple to construct.

The more modest Upland South and Creole folk types continued to be built, and served as dwellings for many Louisianians outside of New Orleans. In the Florida Parishes, for example, the pen tradition persisted until the 1890s, and the Cajuns of Southwest Louisiana continued to build their Creole houses until the turn of the century.

Those great plantation houses that survived the War, however, were never duplicated. They either slowly disintegrated until all that remained was a double row of live oaks leading to crumbling columns, or, like their Natchez brethren, quietly awaited restoration. The few substantial houses that were built in New Orleans during the years surrounding 1870 were mostly built in New Orleans. Despite the ever-present poverty, and unlike the rest of the South, New Orleans recovered economically during Reconstruction, and new housing in parts of the city stands as testimony.[18]

The national architectural styles whose periods of popularity overlapped in 1870 were the Gothic Revival (1840-1880), Italianate (1840-1885), Exotic Revivals (1835-ca. 1890), Second Empire (1855-

1885), and Stick (1860-ca. 1890). Because the period of Reconstruction predates the era of inexpensive and abundant architectural detailing that could be purchased at the nearby lumberyard and easily attached to existing buildings, examples of structures exhibiting these styles were probably built contemporaneous to the style's national popularity.

As noted earlier, most examples of Gothic Revival in Louisiana are antebellum. The latter half of the style's national popularity coincides with the Civil War and Reconstruction, and, according to the McAlesters, these events "all but halted building until the waning days of Gothic influence."[19]

The Italianate style was a little longer lived in Louisiana, but once again the period of the 1860s and early 1870s was the nadir of building in Louisiana, and most examples of this style in the state are antebellum. Nevertheless, a very late example of this style can be seen in the Plaquemines Parish Courthouse, which was built in 1890 in Pointe-a-la-Hache.

The Exotic Revival style has three main types: Egyptian, Oriental, and Swiss Chalet. They are extremely rare everywhere in the country, and especially rare in the South. Louisiana has little Exotic Revival domestic architecture, but the author has seen large mausoleums in the Egyptianate style in the Metairie cemetery and the Grace Episcopal Church cemetery in St. Francisville. In fact, Egyptianate Revival as an architectural style is probably more familiar to Americans in the memorial rather than in the domestic context. The Egyptian-inspired obelisk is a seemingly ubiquitous form in American cemeteries, and considered especially appropriate for the most visible example of public architecture in our nation's capital: the Washington Monument.[20]

Comparatively little of the Second Empire style was built in Louisiana. The surviving examples were mostly constructed in New Orleans after the Civil War.[21] This architectural style is actually most common in the Northeast and Midwest, and Southern examples are relatively rare.

The final architectural style of the Reconstruction time period, the Stick style, is transitional between Gothic Revival and Queen Anne. It begins at the same time as the Civil War so Louisianians had little opportunity to build in this style until a modicum of economic recovery returned to the state sometime in the 1870s. In a few short years, however, the style that would be the hallmark of the railroad and lumber boom, Queen Anne, completely eclipsed the Stick style.

In general, the Reconstruction period was truly a low point in the architectural history of the state. Folk housing continued to be the mainstay of domestic architecture. The period of the plantation house had passed. And, the comparatively few "styled" houses that were built in 1870 were most likely in New Orleans.

9. The Railroad and Lumber Boom

The symbiotic spread of rail transportation and the growth of the lumber industry gained such a momentum in Louisiana beginning in 1890 that it can best be described as a "boom." The railroad and lumber boom of Louisiana, which continued into the twentieth century, is an important juncture in the historical geography of the state because it facilitated initial occupation of land, accelerated the growth of many land-locked towns, and served as a harbinger of culture change. This chapter, therefore, assesses the significance of the railroad and lumber boom to the settlement geography of the state at the close of the nineteenth century.

Although the railroad as a mode of transport and commercial lumbering had each been present in Louisiana prior to 1890, it was their post-Reconstruction synergism that created the boom and brought Louisiana out of its social and economic slump of the last three decades. It was not until after the Civil War that the railroad became a serious contender for part of the transportation market, vying with the steamboat. And, Louisiana's forests were not exploited to the extent that even by the time of the Civil War the state was still roughly 75% forested; that, despite a large portion of the state devoted to agriculture.

Louisianians embraced the railroad as a useful technological innovation as quickly and readily as anyone in the world; the world's first rail line was built in England in 1825 to service the coal industry and within a decade six railroads in Louisiana were chartered or incorporated. These were the Pontchartrain Railroad (1830), the West Feliciana Railroad (1831), the Clinton-Port Hudson Railroad (1833), the New Orleans and Carrollton Railroad (1833), the Alexandria and Cheneyville Railroad (1833), and the New Orleans and Nashville Railroad (1835). Later rail lines included the Mexican Gulf (1837), the New Orleans, Jackson and Great Northern (1850), and the Vicksburg, Shreveport and Texas (1852).

Despite the early optimism and enthusiasm for railroads and the rapidity with which companies formed and made plans, most routes only existed as lines on the map rather than on the landscape until well after the Civil War. The dormancy of the railroad in Louisiana can be attributed to the supremacy and entrenchment of the steamboat and the dominance of the plantation system that endorsed it. Building a railroad was a laborious task requiring a significant capital investment, and most of the wealth in the state was in the hands of planters who were, in general, well situated with regard to water transportation and satisfied with the existing system. According to historian R.S. Cotterill, "railroads were looked upon as auxiliaries to the rivers rather than as main lines of transportation."[1] As a result, in the three decades between the first Louisiana railroad charter and the outbreak of the Civil War, the combined effort of the ten railroad companies just cited was slightly over ten miles of new track per year. This is not exactly a flurry of railroad-building activity!

The real period of railroad construction occurred in the wake of Reconstruction. Essentially nothing got done from 1860 to 1880. Later railroads differed from their antebellum counterparts in two important respects: they were considered to be more than simply adjunct to water transport, and they were controlled by Northern business interests.

The most successful early railroad was the New Orleans, Jackson and Great Northern, later called the Illinois Central Railroad. It eventually connected the Gulf and the Great Lakes, with termini at New Orleans and Chicago. Writing in 1874, geographer Samuel Lockett referred to this as the most important rail line in the state and "second only to the Mississippi River as a means of inter-communication between the metropolis of the South [New Orleans] and the other states of the Union."[2]

The importance of this route was given political recognition in Louisiana in 1869 by the creation of a new parish—Tangipahoa. The linear form of Tangipahoa Parish paralleling the Illinois Central the entire north-south distance of this portion of the Florida Parishes, and the settlement pattern closely aligned to that route, has prompted one geographer to refer to Tangipahoa Parish as "the child of the Illinois Central."[3]

In 1874, Lockett mentioned four railroads of any consequence and some miscellaneous lines in operation in the state.[4] In all, they amounted to four hundred miles of track. The Louisiana portion of the New Orleans, Jackson and Great Northern Railroad was fully functioning. The Mobile, New Orleans and Texas Railroad ran east from New Orleans to Mobile and west as far as Donaldsonville. The Morgan's Louisiana and Texas Railroad was operational between New Orleans and Morgan City. And, the only completed portion of the North Louisiana and Texas Railroad was between Delta, a town on the Mississippi across from Vicksburg, and Monroe.

Some eighteen years after Lockett described the status of railroads in the state, George Cram published his *Railroad and County Map of Louisiana*.[5] One of the most immediate observations made when comparing the two sources is that the amount of railroad track had dramatically increased. In fact, it had more than tripled, from 400 miles to 1,300 miles. Lengthy expanses of rail lines now traversed the state. The major east-west route across North Louisiana, whose name had changed to the Vicksburg, Shreveport and Pacific, was complete. The Texas Pacific cut a diagonal swath through the state linking New Orleans, Alexandria, and Shreveport. And, the old Morgan's Louisiana and Texas had pushed beyond Morgan City and ran northwest through

Lafayette to connect with the Texas Pacific in Cheneyville, as well as providing a link with the Galveston Harbor and San Antonio Railroad, now the Southern Pacific, which ran west from Lafayette.

The development of the lumbering industry in Louisiana goes back a great deal further than that of railroads. Whereas railroads developed slowly for approximately half a century beginning in 1830, the state's forest resources were used on a commercial basis, albeit on a relatively small scale, since the beginning of colonial settlement.[6] Logging activity for the entire period prior to the Civil War was confined to areas where logs could be rafted on rivers to mill or market. The expanding net of rail lines ushered in a whole new period in logging technology that is frequently referred to as "industrial lumbering."[7]

Some historians of the lumber industry in Louisiana divide it into three time periods.[8] Each period is defined by transportation technology. In the initial period logging was confined to small plots of land adjacent to streams that could be used to raft logs to mill and market. The next phase corresponded to Louisiana's lumber boom, and was significantly more intensive and took full advantage of the railroad. The final and present phase, now associated with log trucks and road-building equipment, is synonymous with modern forestry practices in the state.

The important factor in these three phases is transportation. Increasing flexibility in log transport allowed for greater resource exploitation. The middle phase was made possible because of the relative ease of establishing trunk rail lines to all forested areas of the state except the cypress swamp. The West Point-trained engineer Samuel Lockett, in fact, writing during Reconstruction, advocated expansion of the railroad into the forested uplands and saw few impediments in the terrain. "All of the upland country is well timbered; the streams are not large or difficult to bridge; and in no part of the state will be encountered any serious trouble in making excavations and embankments in preparing a road bed."[9]

The railroad, therefore, was clearly a catalyst for logging in the state; so much so that some see it as a *sine qua non* for the period of industrial logging. According to geographer George Stokes, "railroad expansion was essential to forest exploitation."[10] Historian Nollie Hickman, speaking of the eastern Florida Parishes, stated, "commercial lumbering in the back country of east Louisiana received a powerful stimulus with the construction of the New Orleans, Jackson and Great Northern Railroad."[11] Davis added, "during the 1890's, after the completion of the Kansas City Southern Railroad, the western section of the state rapidly developed its lumber industry."[12]

The railroad and lumber boom stimulated the growth of settlement in the forested interior areas of the state, and is especially credited with the creation of numerous towns. As rails penetrated mature stands of timber, towns, however ephemeral, sprang up seemingly overnight. Many of these towns followed a familiar boom and bust cycle.[13] Nevertheless, a surprising number of these "sawmill towns," such as Bernice in Union Parish, Dubach in Lincoln Parish, Alden Bridge in Bossier Parish, Fisher in Sabine Parish, and Elizabeth in Allan Parish, survived to the present.

The railroad and lumber town was incredibly prosperous for a time. Bernice in 1899, for example, sold $7,000 worth of house lots in one day.[14] With the sawmills of these towns turning out tens of thousands of board feet of lumber each day the railroads were kept busy hauling this valuable commodity to market and bringing in scores of workers and a wide range of goods. The typical town boasted elegant hotels, churches serving various congregations, a business district parallel or perpendicular to the railroad line itself, and neighborhoods with large mansions of company officials and prosperous merchants, as well as those of the workers who lived in rows of company-built housing. The prosperity was fleeting, however, and in two to three decades many of these towns disappeared.

The industrial lumbering period lasted from about 1890 to almost 1930. Because of a policy of "cut out and get out," the big logging companies added Louisiana to their list of states that had been denuded to satisfy an appetite for American virgin timber.[15] The pace of this consumption was incredible indeed. Loggers working for some of the big sawmills could, like so many gypsy moths eating their way through a forest, devour an entire section, one square mile, of virgin timber in two weeks or less.[16]

Just as the railroad helped create the period of industrial lumbering and its attendant settlement, so too it stimulated a significant period of settlement in a non-forested region of the state: the prairie.[17] In 1885, railroad and land company interests hired the noted Iowa State University professor of agriculture, Dr. Seaman A. Knapp, and asked him to assess the agricultural potential of the prairie region of Southwest Louisiana. After careful study he determined that rice would be the best crop for this region's climate, terrain, and soil. Upon Knapp's recommendation, large numbers of grain farmers from the American Midwest were given free passage on the railroad to come to the Southwest prairies to see for themselves the prospects of this new agricultural region. A large number of farmers accepted the offer and decided to immigrate to Louisiana. As a result, many of the cultural landscape elements of the Midwest are replicated in Southwest Louisiana.[18] According to Newton, "Roads are oriented on the cardinal directions, fields are square conforming to the sections of the township-and-range system, land is tilled to its edges, and towns are grids straddling railroads."[19]

Generally, the placement of towns along the railroad was not a haphazard event; railroad company engineers made those decisions. One such planned town was Crowley, along the Southern Pacific Railroad on the prairies west of Lafayette. Crowley, the parish seat of Acadia Parish, was founded in 1887 and named for an employee of the Southern Pacific Railroad.[20] Other planned towns in this part of the state include Oberlin, Kinder, Jennings, and Iowa.

The railroad and lumber boom, therefore, significantly furthered the viability and intensity of settlement to include the heretofore sparsely populated longleaf pine forests, shortleaf pine forests, flatwoods, and southwestern prairies. The so-called piney woods portions of Louisiana in 1890 were, for the first time, making the transition from pioneer self-sufficiency to participation in a national economy. One might even say that industrial lumbering effectively closed the chapter on the Upland South frontier period. The railroad was also responsible for much of the initial settlement of the prairies of Southwest Louisiana.

The creation of most of the new parishes in the two decades preceding 1890 reflect, to a degree, population growth in the piney woods and prairies of northern, western, and southwestern Louisiana. The six new parishes created between 1870 and 1890 were Webster, Lincoln, Red River, Carroll split into East and West, Vernon, and Acadia.

The number of towns and cities with a population greater than one thousand had more than doubled. New Orleans retained its crown as primate city with 242,039 residents according to the 1890 census. Shreveport was the second largest urban place in the state with a population of 11,979, edging out the capital—Baton Rouge—by 1,501. Some of these towns with populations over one thousand had significantly fewer residents twenty years earlier. Their growth can be attributed to the railroad and lumber boom. They were, to name a few, Lake Charles (3,442), Morgan City (2,291), Franklin (2,127), Lafayette (2,106), Amite (1,510), Patterson (1,414), Minden (1,298), and Homer (1,132).

A good example of the difference a railroad can make in the prosperity of a town is supplied by comparing two towns, both parish seats along the Bayou Teche: New Iberia and St. Martinville. In 1870, their populations were about equal, with New Iberia having 1,472 residents and St. Martinville having 1,190. The Southern Pacific Railroad went through New Iberia and bypassed St. Martinville. The 1890 census reveals that while New Iberia had more than doubled and now had a population of 3,447, St. Martinville only had 624 new residents.

One example of growth on the parish level attributed to the railroad and lumber boom is Calcasieu Parish. The parish's 1870 population was

6,773, while by the 1890 census it had risen to 20,176. This represents a threefold increase in the intervening twenty years. By way of comparison, East Baton Rouge Parish, containing the state capital, went from 17,816 to 25,922, or an increase of only one and a half during the same interval. In terms of real numbers, Calcasieu Parish gained by 13,443, while East Baton Rouge Parish gained by only 8,106.

The railroad and lumber boom is an important period in the historical settlement geography of Louisiana. From the wider perspective that the passage of time provides, it represents one of those significant punctuations in the evolution of a culture. Industrial lumbering brought a return to economic prosperity the likes of which had not been seen for two generations. Louisianians were learning to parlay their natural resources into tangible income, an adaptation that would manifest itself in the twentieth and twenty-first centuries (e.g., oil and gas revenue). And, with the establishment of Midwestern farmers in Southwest Louisiana the complexion of commercial agriculture in the state was also changing. This change was so dramatic that it prompted Post to argue that the mechanized rice industry in Southwest Louisiana represented "a type of agriculture in which white men would do most of the work—a departure from a generally established custom in the South."[21] Finally, the revolution in transportation initiated by the railroad meant that Louisianians were able to break away from their hereditary reliance on the naturally imposed pattern of navigable waterways. This permitted and encouraged the settlement of interfluve areas of the state where places such as Ruston, founded in 1884 and now Louisiana's eighteenth largest city, were established and continue to prosper into the twenty-first century.

Building Diversity and Proliferation

Geographer Milton Newton noted that, "between 1880 and 1920, the architectural landscape of both town and country in the State was completely overhauled."[22] This statewide facelift was actually part of a national architectural transformation brought about by the railroad and lumber boom. The McAlesters observed, "Rail transportation made inexpensive building materials—principally lumber from large mills located in timber-rich areas—readily available over much of the nation."[23]

Because Louisiana fully participated in the railroad and lumber boom it is not surprising to see the extent of modification of the cultural landscape. These landscape changes came in the form of newly built structures and alterations of older structures. The architectural impact of the railroad and lumber boom on modern landscape perception is so profound, in fact, that people tend to think of a Victorian structure, for example, as an old house. But, as Newton pointed out, "much of the historic landscape of Louisiana came down to us as the remains of the dawn of technical order, the New South, not the traditional South of romance."[24]

There are four recognized folk and vernacular house types typical of the railroad and lumber boom: the Midwest I-house, the bungalow, the pyramidal house, and a variant of the shotgun, the North Shore house. Although the historical genesis of some of these types is a little obscure, particularly the bungalow, they are best placed within the architectural legacy of the railroad and lumber boom. Certainly the Midwest I-house belongs to this time-slice. The pyramidal house was a common type of workers' housing in mill towns and is representative of the period. And, the North Shore house is clearly a Victorian architectural phenomenon.

The Midwest I-house is a type common to the prairie region of Southwest Louisiana. It is simply two rooms wide, one room deep, and two stories high. There is often a one-story ell. The Midwest I-house lacks a central hall and full-length gallery.

Just as the Carolina I-house is testimony to a migration of people from the Carolinas, the Midwest I-house is evidence on the cultural landscape of a migration of people from the Midwest.[25] These Midwesterners came to Louisiana in the late nineteenth century following the "opening up" of the prairies by the railroads.

The bungalow house is a late nineteenth and early twentieth century form that, at first glance, appears to be a double shotgun, but there is no clear evidence that the shotgun and bungalow are related forms.[26] A common floor plan is two rooms wide and three rooms deep. The bungalow house is primarily a single-family dwelling, but some are used as rental duplexes. The house *type* should not be confused with the architectural *style*.

The pyramidal house is simply a square of four rooms with a pyramidal roof. Chimneys can be either interior or exterior. Porches, if present, are not a major architectural element. Additions in the form of an ell, if present, are generally at the back, although it is not uncommon for one to be located in the front. This type is found in all parts of the state, but there is a significant concentration of pyramidal houses in Southwest Louisiana. Pyramidal houses are also found with some frequency in former sawmill towns, for example Kentwood in Tangipahoa Parish. Built in cookie-cutter fashion, they form rows of identical houses that bear the unmistakable mark of company-built housing. Kniffen has described the workmen's quarters of a sawmill town as, "monotonous rows of square, one-storied, pyramidal-roofed houses."[27] This type seems to be related to the popular national type known as the "American four square."[28]

The North Shore house is a "T" plan shotgun with wrap-around galleries. Some of the more affluent residents of New Orleans built these houses on the north shore of Lake Pontchartrain as second homes in order to escape the oppressive summers of that city.[29] They were built with some frequency in southern St. Tammany Parish in such places as Abita Springs and Mandeville. The North Shore house type usually displays some architectural style such as Queen Anne.

The railroad and lumber boom was also the period of architectural style. It crosscuts more periods of architectural style popularity than any other time-slice in this book. The period of 1870 is a close second, but given the general economic conditions of the time, actual Louisiana examples of styles then popular (nationally) are comparatively few.

The proximity of sawmills, inexpensive and architecturally adaptable balloon framing, and efficient rapid transportation contributed to the spread of "styled" houses in Louisiana in the 1890s.

Concomitant with material and transportation was the important factor known to cultural geographers as the rise of popular culture. Architectural style, from the folk cultural perspective, was once viewed as only for elite residences and civic and religious buildings. This view is still held by some architectural historians. Architectural style became a component of popular culture in the 1890s by being advertised in magazines, sold piecemeal at the local lumberyard, and integrated into rapidly growing cities and towns.

The architectural styles that were nationally popular during the period of the railroad and lumber boom in Louisiana spanned from the end of the Second Empire and Stick styles, 1885 and 1890 respectively, through the period of popularity of the California Bungalow, which ended around 1930. Of these eleven styles, the Queen Anne style (1880-1910) was probably the most popular in Louisiana in 1890. The Queen Anne style, which actually includes the variety commonly called Eastlake, was the most popular style for domestic architecture for the last two decades of the nineteenth century, and the New South of the railroad and lumber boom has some of the most elegant examples.[30]

It is particularly common for Queen Anne style to be expressed structurally as well as decoratively. More elaborate specimens of the Queen Anne style were constructed with towers, projecting gables and bay windows, porches, and an overall asymmetrical appearance. Complex Queen Anne Victorian houses were generally designed by architects, but folk and vernacular examples did not usually require building a whole new structure to accommodate the style; stylistic elements were simply added to the facades of folk and vernacular buildings. This added style came in the form of decorative details, and functioned largely as a visual enhancement.

Another style of the Victorian period, named for the Louisiana-born architect, Henry Hobson Richardson (1838-1886), is the Richardsonian

Romanesque. After studying architecture at Harvard and the Ecole des Beaux-Arts in Paris, he worked in New York and eventually settled in Boston where he designed some of his best known buildings.[31] These buildings consisted of massive masonry and stone construction with elaborate towers and arches, and, as a consequence, were extremely labor intensive and expensive to build. The style is usually associated with civic architecture such as libraries, schools, and courthouses. In Louisiana, an example of this style can be seen in the Pointe Coupee Parish Courthouse in New Roads, which was completed in 1902.

The Colonial Revival style is said to have grown out of the Philadelphia Centennial in 1876 that stimulated interest in the architecture of the colonial Eastern Seaboard. It consists of a rather free interpretation of structural and stylistic elements of colonial houses, often resulting in a composite colonial-looking, frequently Georgian, house. The Colonial Revival style is an eclectic category of architectural style with a relatively long period of popularity.

Like the Colonial Revival, the Neoclassical style is also a long-lived eclectic architectural style. One of the hallmarks of this style, according to the McAlesters, is a "façade dominated by a full-height porch with roof supported by classical columns."[32] The Neoclassical was particularly popular in the New South where a penchant for columned architecture existed. Louisianians, for example, appropriately selected the Neoclassical style for the official home of their governor, now the old Governor's Mansion, built in the 1930s. It later became very popular in some subdivisions attempting to appear "upscale."

The Beaux Arts style is a turn-of-the-century architectural style that exudes wealth through its massive stone or masonry construction and ornate detailing.[33] Some of the best public architectural examples of this style, such as the Library of Congress, are found in the nation's capital. Domestic examples in the Beaux Arts style were designed by architects and tend to be located in wealthy neighborhoods in urban contexts.[34] Louisiana public architectural examples of the style include the Beauregard Parish Courthouse (1914) in De Ridder and the Whitney National Bank (1909) in New Orleans.

The Mission Revival was to the West what the Colonial Revival was to the East. It began in California around 1890 and represents an architectural adaptation of the state's many Spanish colonial missions. And, according to the McAlesters, "it received further impetus when the Santa Fe and Southern Pacific railways adopted the style for stations and resort hotels throughout the West."[35] Many examples of the Mission Revival style in Louisiana undoubtedly owe their existence to the inspiration of the railroad. Mission Revival style railroad stations in Louisiana include depots in Acadia, Calcasieu, and Vernon parishes.

The Prairie style, unlike the other styles mentioned, explicitly avoided an architectural revival or replication of classical, medieval, or romantic forms. The Prairie style originated in Chicago around the turn of the century and is associated with the architect Frank Lloyd Wright. Wright and others attempted to design an architectural interpretation of the rolling landform of the American Midwest. The style was somewhat popular between 1900 and 1920 in the Upper Midwest, but according to Poppeliers, Chambers, and Schwartz, "during the first decades of the 20th century most Americans chose to live, work and shop in buildings patterned after architectural styles of the past."[36]

There can be no greater contrast in American architecture of the early twentieth century than the difference between the general public rejection of the Prairie style and their overwhelming embrace of the California Bungalow style. So popular was the Bungalow style, in fact, that magazines devoted entirely to the style flourished, and one could even receive by mail order a California Bungalow style house through the Sears catalog. It was probably the first architectural style fully embraced by the common man, an architectural phenomenon followed later in the twentieth century by the rapid and widespread diffusion of the Ranch house. Newton observed that, "any town in Louisiana that was prospering at all between 1890 and 1930 has whole neighborhoods of California bungalow houses and other types trimmed with elements of that style."[37] Further, the California Bungalow style is strictly a domestic architectural style, whereas even the Prairie style, for example, found expression in civic architecture such as banks and courthouses.

In sum, from the beginning of the railroad and lumber boom to the present, Louisianians have been increasingly participatory in popular culture. Concern with architectural style—fashion or fad, if you prefer—has been a component of this. Some who could afford to do so built full-blown examples of the style then popular. And, these newly constructed stylish houses often clustered in expanding neighborhoods.

10. Historic Preservation in the Bayou State

Louisiana is a unique place—from its architecture to its zydeco music. Professionals in a variety of academic disciplines, as well as informed non-professionals, participate in the study and preservation of the state's cultural heritage.[1] Nationally, this effort is subsumed under the rubric of historic preservation. One active and vital branch of historic preservation concerns itself with the so-called "built environment," or historic standing structures. This branch is the traditional domain of the architectural historian, but, as this book endeavors to point out, it is an area where others can and should contribute.

Historical geographers, because of their ability to place cultural phenomena in the appropriate spatial and temporal dimension, produce research that can significantly benefit the frequently parallel interests of the preservationist. They accomplish this by modeling the past, determining historical human-environment relationships, studying landscape change, and inventorying relict features of the extant cultural landscape. This book has addressed each of these with specific reference to Louisiana of the eighteenth and nineteenth centuries.

The settlement history of Louisiana may appear at first glance to be a chaotic blend of French, African, Spanish, British, and American occupation of an extremely heterogeneous physical environment. The only way to conceptualize the contributions of its citizens over a period of roughly two hundred years—hewing timbers, building levees, chopping cotton, producing Tabasco brand pepper sauce, and a variety of other activities—is through abstraction. This historical geography of the settlement of Louisiana, therefore, is a generalization of these countless historical activities.

In many respects, the settlement of Louisiana mirrors that of the Anglo-American Eastern United States where settlement was confined to relatively concentrated core areas for most of the colonial period. Until the American statehood period, Louisianians lived in a definite core area in the south with a few scattered outposts in the north and west. The nineteenth century American period in Louisiana, like the country as a whole, is characterized by an onslaught of eager settlers who filled in the gaps.

The question of historical human-environment relationships is a significant contextual component of this book. Constant reference is made throughout to the correspondence between settlement and the state's various environments. Any map of Louisiana's potential natural vegetation illustrates, for example, the overwhelming importance of the bottomlands (natural levee) environment to plantation agriculture. The concept of the human-environment relationship, which is central to historical geography, is well illustrated in Louisiana's physical and cultural diversity. Cattle ranches and irrigated rice farms thrived on the prairies. Northern lumber companies were drawn like a magnet to Louisiana's magnificent longleaf and shortleaf pine forests. Pirates found refuge in the labyrinth of bays and rivers that cut into the coastal marsh. Grecian columns and sugarcane sprang up from the rich alluvial bottomlands.

Because these human-environment relationships were not static, but dynamic and changing, this book addresses landscape change. The device used to describe and assess Louisiana's cultural landscapes over time is the time-slice. Each of seven time-slices is composed of two parts: the first part presents the patterns and processes of the human-environment relationship that are most characteristic of the period, and the second specifically deals with the housing types and architectural styles that also typify that particular time-slice.

The appreciation gained by presenting buildings in their spatial and temporal contexts comes from a fuller understanding of the structure's place in the cultural landscape. For example, to grasp the true historical significance of the antebellum plantation home one must see it not as an isolated entity, but as part of a larger system that included land, slaves, factors, steamboats, politics, architects, and so forth. All these actors and activities functioned within definite spatial and temporal parameters.

Old houses, like any other item of material culture, can profitably be thought of from a theoretical perspective as artifacts—a kind of fossilized human behavior. Just as the archaeologist sees a functioning culture in an assemblage of stone tools and fragments of pottery, the historical geographer understands that our relict cultural landscape needs to be interpreted from the perspective of the past. This book attempts to identify some of the more important elements that played a part in the creation of the cultural landscape. For example, the very existence of some towns and cities in Louisiana, not to mention architecture, can be credited to the impact of the steamboat and the railroad. This book, within the framework of the time-slice, isolates the more important physical and cultural variables that need to be considered in conjunction with historic standing structures to achieve a holistic view of the past.

The most important contribution that this book makes to historic preservation is its demonstration that the perspective of the historical geographer can enhance our understanding of historic standing structures by concentrating, to a large extent, on the milieu of which they were once a part. In a separate publication, the author examined the relationships of land claims from the colonial period with potential natural vegetation and historic domestic architecture and found, as one would expect, significant correlation.[2] Geography has often been described as the academic discipline that studies the "why" of "where," and this book has gone to some lengths to do just that with respect to historic standing architecture.

With the relict cultural landscape either slipping away gradually by attrition and neglect or disappearing in an instant by demolition or natural disaster, some difficult decisions must be made. How to manage the state's architectural heritage, especially in view of a disaster on the scale of Hurricane Katrina, is of primary concern to the historic preservationist.

One issue brought to the fore by Hurricane Katrina is the biased record of Louisiana structures on the National Register of Historic Places. Until recently, one could examine the individually listed structures (as opposed to historic districts) and recognize immediately the overwhelming presence of the Greek Revival style.[3] The 1850 time-slice suggested that this architectural style was extremely popular, but with so many Greek Revival homes on the National Register it is clear that the selection process is other than representative.

One key to the plethora of Greek Revival structures on the National Register is probably found in the local and state nomination process. There is little doubt that in the hearts and minds of many Louisianians the antebellum plantation house, "preferably white and with columns and Grecian entablature," is a tangible architectural symbol of the zenith of Southern civilization, and therefore deserving of National Register recognition.[4] The architectural and historical merits of the Greek Revival and the antebellum plantation home are not in question here. What seems evident is that those who select historic structures in Louisiana for national recognition have had a relatively narrow focus when it comes to the state's heterogeneous cultural landscape.

Since its establishment in 1966, the National Register of Historic Places has not functioned as a repository of representative or ordinary historic cultural resources, although the criteria for eligibility are sufficiently broad so as to apply to most structures older than fifty years and in reasonably good condition.[5] In practice, the National Register's listing of historic structures has tended to concentrate on more "high style" examples. This tendency, therefore, partially explains the dominance of Louisiana's Greek Revival architecture on a nationally recognized scale.

The catastrophic damage done to Southeast Louisiana in 2005 has rekindled an interest in what one geographer has termed "ordinary landscapes."[6] Appreciation of what has been lost, as well as what remains, is as much a matter of context as it is material form. That is the *raison d'être* of this book. Louisiana's incomparable built environment is a part of the present and a tangible link to the past. It is a significant component of a cultural identity made all the more valuable in light of what author James Conaway calls "vanishing America."[7]

One positive outcome of Hurricane Katrina is the reaffirmation of an inscription in front of the National Archives in Washington, D.C.: "What is Past is Prologue." Apropos to Louisiana after the storm, it is from Shakespeare's play, *The Tempest*. The same sentiment is implicit in the fabric of every old building, great and small, in the Bayou State.

Notes

1. Time, Space, and Houses

1. A brief perusal of the bibliography should offer a sense of the range of published and unpublished sources available to the student of Louisiana's built environment.

2. Two classic works by the same author—Ralph Brown—illustrate the distinction between synchronic and diachronic historical studies. Ralph H. Brown, *Mirror for Americans: Likeness of the Eastern Seaboard, 1810* (New York: American Geographical Society, 1943), and *Historical Geography of the United States* (New York: Harcourt, Brace, 1948).

3. Derwent Whittlesey, "Sequent Occupance" *Annals of the Association of American Geographers* 19 (1929): 162; Richard Hartshorne, *The Nature of Geography* (Lancaster, PA: Association of American Geographers, 1949), 184.

4. Andrew H. Clark, "Historical Geography," in *American Geography: Inventory and Prospect*, Preston E. James and Clarence F. Jones, eds. (Syracuse, NY: Syracuse University Press, 1954), 71.

5. Punctuated equilibrium is currently a viable theoretical paradigm in studies of hominid evolution. Although the evidence is scant, the fossil record seems to indicate that human morphological change was not a slow and continuous process. Phylogenesis occurred, according to this view, in periodic episodes followed by relative ontogenic stability.

6. Whittlesey, "Sequent Occupance," 162. Emphasis mine.
7. Marvin W. Mikesell, "The Rise and Decline of 'Sequent Occupance:' A Chapter in the History of American Geography," in *Geographies of the Mind*, David Lowenthal and Martyn J. Bowden, eds. (New York: Oxford University Press, 1976), 161.
8. Jan O.M. Broek, *The Santa Clara Valley, California: A Study in Landscape Changes* (Utrecht, The Netherlands: Utrecht University, 1932).
9. Jan O.M. Broek, *Geography: Its Scope and Spirit* (Columbus, OH: Charles E. Merrill, 1965), 29.
10. Fred B. Kniffen, "Why Folk Housing?" *Annals of the Association of American Geographers* 69 (1979): 60.
11. James F. Deetz, *Invitation to Archaeology* (New York: Natural History Press, 1967), 45-46.
12. In American archaeology, opposing sides of this issue are best represented by James A. Ford and Albert C. Spaulding. See Gordon R. Willey and Jeremy A. Sabloff, *A History of American Archaeology* (San Francisco: W.H. Freeman, 1993), 165.
13. Fred B. Kniffen, "Louisiana House Types," *Annals of the Association of American Geographers* 26 (1936): 179-93.
14. James A. Ford, "The Type Concept Revisited," *American Anthropologist* 56 (1954): 42-54.
15. Robert W. Neuman, *An Introduction to Louisiana Archaeology* (Baton Rouge: Louisiana State University Press, 1984), 46-47.
16. Milton B. Newton, Jr. and Linda Pulliam-DeNapoli, "Log Houses as Public Occasions: A Historical Theory," *Annals of the Association of American Geographers* 67 (1977): 360.
17. Gordon R. Willey and Philip Phillips, *Method and Theory in American Archaeology* (Chicago: University of Chicago Press, 1958), 37.
18. Ibid, 33.
19. Willey and Sabloff, *A History of American Archaeology*, 109.
20. There are quite a few field guides to architectural style styles available. Any list of the most popular and widely applicable would include the following: John J.G. Blumenson, *Identifying American Architecture: A Pictorial Guide to Styles and Terms,*

1600-1945 (Lanham, MD: AltaMira Press, 1981); Virginia McAlester and Lee McAlester, *A Field Guide to American Houses* (New York: Alfred A. Knopf, 1984); and John C. Poppeliers, S. Allen Chambers, Jr., and Nancy B. Schwartz, *What Style is it? A Guide to American Architecture* (Washington, D.C.: The Preservation Press, 1983), as well as the classic, Marcus Whiffen, *American Architecture Since 1780: A Guide to Styles* (Cambridge, MA: M.I.T. Press, 1969). For Louisiana, see Jonathan Fricker, Donna Fricker, and Patricia L. Duncan, *Louisiana Architecture: A Handbook on Styles* (Lafayette: Center for Louisiana Studies, University of Louisiana, 1998), as well as Fred Daspit's three-part series, *Louisiana Architecture: 1714-1820, Louisiana Architecture: 1820-1840,* and *Louisiana Architecture: 1840-1860* (Lafayette: University of Louisiana, Center for Louisiana Studies, 2005, 2005, and 2007 respectively).

21. *Oxford English Dictionary*, 2nd ed., s.v. "style."
22. McAlester and McAlester, *A Field Guide to American Houses*, 5.
23. Milton B. Newton, Jr., *Louisiana: A Geographical Portrait* (Baton Rouge: Geoforensics, 1987), 172.
24. Poppeliers, Chambers, and Schwartz, *What Style is it?*, 10.
25. Richard Pillsbury and Andrew Kardos, *A Field Guide to the Folk Architecture of the Northeastern United States* (Hanover, NH: Geography Publications at Dartmouth No. 8, 1970), 16.
26. Dell Upton and John M. Vlach, eds., *Common Places: Readings in American Vernacular Architecture* (Athens: University of Georgia Press, 1986), xx.
27. McAlester and McAlester, *A Field Guide to American Houses*, 310.
28. Many dating keys are in print to aid in determining the relative age of a structure. Edwards and Wells, for example, show how nails – wrought, cut, and wire, among others – can be used as chronological indicators. Jay D. Edwards and Tom Wells, *Historic Louisiana Nails: Aids to the Dating of Old Buildings* (Baton Rouge: Geoscience Publications, Department of Geography & Anthropology, Louisiana State University, 1994).

29. Jay D. Edwards, *A Survey of Louisiana French Vernacular Architecture* (Baton Rouge: Louisiana State University, Museum of Geoscience, 1982), 141.
30. I was conducting an historic standing structure survey of Iberville Parish for the Louisiana Division of Historic Preservation.
31. David Stahle, "Tree-Ring Dating of Historic Buildings in Arkansas," *Tree-Ring Bulletin* 39 (1979): 1-28.
32. Milton B. Newton, Jr., "Louisiana House Types: A Field Guide," (*Melanges* No. 2. Baton Rouge: Geoscience Publications, Department of Geography & Anthropology, Louisiana State University, 1971), 4-6.
33. Newton, *Louisiana: A Geographical Portrait*, 180.
34. Terry G. Jordan-Bychkov, *The Upland South: The Making of an American Folk Region and Landscape* (Staunton, VA: Center for American Places, 2003); Terry G. Jordan and Matti Kaups, *The American Backwoods Frontier: An Ethnic and Ecological Interpretation* (Baltimore: Johns Hopkins University Press, 1992).
35. Fred B. Kniffen, "The Physiognomy of Rural Louisiana," *Louisiana History* 4 (1963): 294.
36. Kniffen, "Louisiana House Types," 185.
37. Milton B. Newton, Jr., "Louisiana Folk Houses," in *Louisiana Folklife: A Guide to the State*, Nicholas R. Spitzer, ed. (Baton Rouge: Louisiana Department of Culture, Recreation, and Tourism, 1985), 184.
38. Robert W. Heck, "Building Traditions in the Acadian Parishes," in *The Cajuns: Essays on Their History and Culture*, Glenn R. Conrad, ed. (Lafayette: University of Southwestern Louisiana, 1978), 161.
39. Newton, "Louisiana Folk Houses," 183.
40. Newton, *Louisiana: A Geographical Portrait*, 189.
41. The most-often cited is the so-called "African house" on the grounds of Melrose Plantation in Natchitoches Parish. See Gary B. Mills, *The Forgotten People: Cane River's Creoles of Color* (Baton Rouge: Louisiana State University Press, 1977), plate following 54, 70.

42. Lawrence E. Estaville, "The Louisiana French Culture Region: Geographic Morphologies in the Nineteenth Century" (Ph.D. diss., University of Oklahoma, 1984).

2. Environmental Diversity in the Bayou State

1. A.W. Kuchler, *Potential Natural Vegetation of the Coterminious United States*, American Geographical Society, Special Publication No. 36, 1964.
2. Harry Jacobs, *Natural Vegetation Map of Louisiana* (Baton Rouge: Louisiana State Board of Engineers, 1937); Lauren C. Post, "Samuel Henry Lockett (1837-1891) – A Sketch of his Life and Work," *Louisiana History* 5 (1964): 421-41.
3. Milton B. Newton, Jr., *Atlas of Louisiana* (Baton Rouge: Geoscience Publications, Department of Geography & Anthropology, Louisiana State University, 1972), 35; Fred B. Kniffen and Sam B. Hilliard, *Louisiana: Its Land and People* (Baton Rouge: Louisiana State University Press, 1988), 79; Terry L. Jones, *The Louisiana Journey* (Layton, UT: Gibbs Smith, 2007), 26.
4. Robert H. Chabreck and Greg Linscombe, *Vegetative Type Map of the Louisiana Coastal Marshes* (New Orleans: Louisiana Department of Wildlife and Fisheries, 1978).
5. The map of Louisiana potential natural vegetation compiled by the author using a series of 1:250,000 scale base maps appeared in *The Professional Geographer* (1993). This was done at the CADGIS Research Laboratory at Louisiana State University in Baton Rouge.
6. According to Newton, the structural approach rests on "the observed fact that similar environments have *similar looking* vegetations. Rain forests, coniferous forests, and prairies look similar, regardless of where they occur. At the same time, similar processes and conditions exist in places where similar vegetation structures occur." Milton B. Newton, Jr., *Louisiana: A Geographical Portrait* (Baton Rouge: Geoforensics, 1987), 73.

7. Thomas C. Nelson and Walter M. Zillgitt, *A Forest Atlas of the South* (United States Department of Agriculture, Forest Service, Southern Forest Experiment Station, New Orleans, 1969), 9.

8. Clair Brown, *Louisiana Trees and Shrubs* (Baton Rouge: Louisiana Commission of Forestry, 1945), 9; Newton, *Louisiana: A Geographical Portrait*, 78.

9. Frequently cited explanations include the presence of a hard clay pan roughly one foot below the surface, and even intentional periodic burning of vegetation by Native Americans in prehistoric times to create clearings. Kniffen and Hilliard, *Louisiana: Its Land and People*, 81; Lauren C. Post, *Cajun Sketches from the Prairies of Southwest Louisiana* (Baton Rouge: Louisiana State University Press, 1974), 15.

10. Newton, *Louisiana: A Geographical Portrait*, 80.

11. Gay Gomez, *A Wetland Biography: Seasons on Louisiana's Chenier Plain* (Austin: University of Texas Press, 1998).

12. Edwin A. Davis, ed. *The Rivers and Bayous of Louisiana* (Baton Rouge: Louisiana Education Research Association, 1968).

13. Gomez, *A Wetland Biography*, 20-22.

14. Kniffen and Hilliard, *Louisiana: Its Land and People*, 54; Richard Campanella, *Geographies of New Orleans: Urban Fabrics Before the Storm* (Lafayette: Center for Louisiana Studies, University of Louisiana, 2006), 36.

15. For an excellent overview of the struggle of the U.S. Army Corps of Engineers versus the Mississippi River's natural inclination to change course and create new outlets to the Gulf of Mexico, see John A. McPhee's essay in *The Control of Nature* (New York: Farrar, Straus, and Giroux, 1990).

3. French Colonial Louisiana

1. Charles Hudson, *The Southeastern Indians* (Knoxville: University of Tennessee Press, 1976), 107-16.

2. Marcel Giraud, *A History of French Louisiana. Volume 1, The Reign of Louis XIV, 1698-1715* (Baton Rouge: Louisiana State University Press, 1953), 31; Francis Parkman, "The French

in Louisiana, 1699-1712" (Ph.D. diss., Harvard University, 1930).

3. Herbert E. Bolton, *The Spanish Borderlands* (New Haven, CT: Yale University Press, 1921).

4. Antoine S. LePage du Pratz, *The History of Louisiana*, Joseph G. Tregle, Jr., ed. (Baton Rouge: Louisiana State University Press, 1975), 27.

5. Patricia D. Woods, "The Relations Between the French of Colonial Louisiana and the Choctaw, Chickasaw, and Natchez, 1699-1762" (Ph.D. diss., Louisiana State University, 1978), 233-34.

6. Craig E. Colten, ed., *Transforming New Orleans and its Environs: Centuries of Change* (Pittsburgh: University of Pittsburgh Press, 2001); Also see Richard Campanella, *Geographies of New Orleans: Urban Fabrics Before the Storm* (Lafayette: Center for Louisiana Studies, University of Louisiana, 2006), 33-87, for a detailed analysis of the city's physical site and situation.

7. Quoted in Samuel Wilson, Jr. *The Vieux Carre, New Orleans, Its Plan, Its Growth, Its Architecture* (The City of New Orleans, Louisiana, 1968), 1.

8. John W. Reps, *Town Planning in Frontier America* (Princeton, NJ: Princeton University Press, 1965), 98.

9. Wilson, *The Vieux Carre*, 6.

10. For example, Quebec City.

11. John G. Clark, *New Orleans, 1718-1812: An Economic History* (Baton Rouge: Louisiana State University Press, 1970), 4.

12. Edwin A. Davis, *Louisiana: A Narrative History* (Baton Rouge: Claitor's Press, 1971), 62-66.

13. J. Hanno Deiler, *The Settlement of the German Coast of Louisiana and the Creoles of German Descent* (Philadelphia: Americana-Germanica Press, 1909).

14. Davis, *Louisiana: A Narrative History*, 58.

15. Woods, "Relations," 1978.

16. Jay D. Edwards, *Louisiana's Remarkable French Vernacular Architecture, 1700-1900* (Baton Rouge: Geoscience Publications, Department of Geography & Anthropology, Louisiana State University, 1988); Jean M. Farnsworth and Ann M. Masson,

eds., *The Architecture of Colonial Louisiana: Collected Essays of Samuel Wilson, Jr.* (Lafayette: Center for Louisiana Studies, University of Louisiana, 1987); Philippe Oszuscik, "French Creole Housing on the Gulf Coast: The Early Years," *Pioneer America Society Transactions* 6 (1983): 49-58.

17. Edwards, *Louisiana's Remarkable French Vernacular Architecture*, 5.

18. Ibid, 5.

19. Ibid, 7.

20. Ibid, 7.

21. Wilson, *The Vieux Carre*, 99.

22. Virginia McAlester and Lee McAlester, *A Field Guide to American Houses* (New York: Alfred A. Knopf, 1984), 120-21.

23. Edwards has developed an elaborate classification system – Class I through Class IIIb – based largely on roof form. Edwards, *Louisiana's Remarkable French Vernacular Architecture*, 4.

24. Ibid, 9.

25. Ignace Francois Brutin, *Plan du Fort des Natcheitoches* (Paris: Archives Nationales, 1733).

26. Fred B. Kniffen, "The Physiognomy of Rural Louisiana," *Louisiana History* 4 (1963): 294; Wilson, *The Vieux Carre*, 99.

27. Edwards, *Louisiana's Remarkable French Vernacular Architecture*, 4.

28. According to Edwards, "in retaining their beloved *pavilion* roof, they produced a distinctive Mississippi Valley French Creole settler's house with a steep inner roof and a sharp break in pitch about halfway between the ridge and the eaves," Jay D. Edwards, "French." In *America's Architectural Roots: Ethnic Groups that Built America*, Dell Upton, ed. (Washington, D.C.: National Trust for Historic Preservation, 1986), 63.

29. Ibid, 64.

4. Spanish and British Colonial Louisiana

1. John P. Moore, *Revolt in Louisiana: The Spanish Occupation, 1766-1770* (Baton Rouge: Louisiana State University Press, 1976).

2. Andrew C. Albrecht, "The Origin and Early Settlement of Baton Rouge, Louisiana," *Louisiana Historical Quarterly* 28 (1945): 5-68; Clarence E. Carter, "The Beginnings of British West Florida," *Mississippi Valley Historical Review* 4 (1917): 314-41; V.M. Seramuzza, "Galveztown, A Spanish Settlement of Colonial Louisiana," *Louisiana Historical Quarterly* 13 (1930): 553-609; Henry Skipwith, *East Feliciana, Louisiana, Past and Present: Sketches of the Pioneers* (New Orleans: Hopkins, 1892).

3. Clinton N. Howard, *The British Development of West Florida, 1763-1769* (Berkeley: University of California Press, 1947).

4. Captain Philip Pittman, *The Present State of European Settlements on the Mississippi*, John F. McDermott, ed. (Memphis, TN: Memphis State University, 1977).

5. Cecil Johnson, *British West Florida, 1763-1783* (New Haven, CT: Yale University Press, 1943), 149.

6. Ibid, 148-149.

7. Henry W. Longfellow, *Evangeline: A Tale of Acadie* (Halifax, Nova Scotia: H.H. Marshall, 1976).

8. Carl A. Brasseaux, *The Founding of New Acadia: The Beginnings of Acadian Life in Louisiana, 1765-1803* (Baton Rouge: Louisiana State University Press, 1987).

9. An arpent is a linear measurement equal to 192 English feet.

10. Jacqueline K. Voorhies, *Some Late Eighteenth Century Louisianians: Census Records of the Colony, 1758-1796* (Lafayette: University of Southwestern Louisiana, 1973), 108.

11. Post states that, "many elements of this pastoral economy undoubtedly were borrowed from the Spanish under whose domination the Acadians lived for more than a third of a century....The prairies were especially suited to the raising of half-wild cattle, and on them the Acadians established their ranches or *vacheries*. Lauren C. Post, *Cajun Sketches from the Prairies of Southwest Louisiana* (Baton Rouge: Louisiana State University Press, 1974, 4.

12. Quoted in David K. Bjork, "Documents Relating to Alexandro O'Reilly and an Expedition sent out by him from New Orleans

to Natchitoches, 1769-1770," *Louisiana Historical Quarterly* 7 (1924): 21.

13. Ibid, 30.

14. Ibid, 31.

15. Ibid, 32-37. Also see Winston De Ville, "Rapides Post on the Red River: Census and Military Documents for Central Louisiana, 1769-1800" (Ville Platte, LA: Privately printed, 1985), 6.

16. Samuel Wilson, Jr. *The Vieux Carre, New Orleans, Its Plan, Its Growth, Its Architecture* (The City of New Orleans, Louisiana, 1968), 44.

17. Edwin A. Davis, *Louisiana: A Narrative History* (Baton Rouge: Claitor's Press, 1971), 109-10.

18. Jay D. Edwards, *Louisiana's Remarkable French Vernacular Architecture, 1700-1900* (Baton Rouge: Geoscience Publications, Department of Geography & Anthropology, Louisiana State University, 1988), 14.

19. Wilson, *The Vieux Carre*, 102.

20. Ibid, 103.

21. Jay D. Edwards, "French." In *America's Architectural Roots: Ethnic Groups that Built America*, Dell Upton, ed. (Washington, D.C.: National Trust for Historic Preservation, 1986), 64. Edwards also notes, "the largest of the raised plantation houses were completely supported by a colonnade of tapered or shaped Tuscan columns crafted from pie-shaped bricks." Edwards, *Louisiana's Remarkable French Vernacular Architecture*, 17.

22. Edwards, *Louisiana's Remarkable French Vernacular Architecture*, 12.

23. Virginia McAlester and Lee McAlester, *A Field Guide to American Houses* (New York: Alfred A. Knopf, 1984), 138-42.

24. Edwards, "French," 64.

25. In addition to the research by the LSU anthropologist Jay D. Edwards cited herein, see Jonathan Fricker, "The Origins of the Creole Raised Plantation House" *Louisiana History* 25 (1984): 137-53; Robert W. Heck, "Building Traditions in the Acadian Parishes" in *The Cajuns: Essays on Their History and Culture*, Glenn R. Conrad, ed. (Lafayette: University of Southwestern Louisiana, 1978), 161-172; Lauren C. Post, *Cajun Sketches from*

the Prairies of Southwest Louisiana (Baton Rouge: Louisiana State University Press, 1974), 83-91.

26. Edwards, *Louisiana's Remarkable French Vernacular Architecture*, 18-21.

27. Milton B. Newton, Jr., "Louisiana House Types: A Field Guide," (*Melanges* No. 2. Baton Rouge: Geoscience Publications, Department of Geography & Anthropology, Louisiana State University, 1971), 14.

28. Edwards, *Louisiana's Remarkable French Vernacular*, 23.

29. Ibid, 28.

5. Territorial Louisiana: Between Colony and Statehood

1. J. Gerald Kennedy, *The Astonished Traveler: William Darby, Frontier Geographer and Man of Letters* (Baton Rouge: Louisiana State University Press, 1981).

2. Edwin A. Davis, *Louisiana: A Narrative History* (Baton Rouge: Claitor's Press, 1971), 157.

3. Norman A. Graebner, Gilbert C. Fite, and Philip L. White, *A History of the American People* (New York: McGraw Hill, 1971), 256.

4. Davis, *Louisiana: A Narrative History*, 165.

5. Harnett T. Kane, *The Bayous of Louisiana* (New York: William Morrow, 1943), 74.

6. Davis, *Louisiana: A Narrative History*, 172-73.

7. Ibid, 173.

8. Marietta M. Lebreton, "History of the Territory of Orleans, 1803-1812" (Ph.D. diss., Louisiana State University, 1969).

9. Davis, *Louisiana: A Narrative History*, 169.

10. John S. Kyser, "The Evolution of Louisiana Parishes in Relation to Population Growth and Movements" (Ph.D. diss., Louisiana State University, 1938), 15.

11. Ibid, 15.

12. Davis, *Louisiana: A Narrative History*, 171.

13. John W. Reps, *Town Planning in Frontier America* (Princeton, NJ: Princeton University Press, 1965), 102.

14. John C. Lewis, "The Settlement Succession of the Boeuf River Basin, Louisiana" (Ph.D. diss., Louisiana State University, 1973), 34.

15. Quoted in Samuel Wilson, Jr. *The Vieux Carre, New Orleans, Its Plan, Its Growth, Its Architecture* (The City of New Orleans, Louisiana, 1968), 112.

16. Ibid, 110.

17. Ibid, 110.

18. Peirce F. Lewis, *New Orleans: The Making of an Urban Landscape* (Cambridge, MA: Ballinger, 1976), 40.

19. John J.G. Blumenson, *Identifying American Architecture: A Pictorial Guide to Styles and Terms, 1600-1945* (Lanham, MD: AltaMira Press, 1981), 20-21; Virginia McAlester and Lee McAlester, *A Field Guide to American Houses* (New York: Alfred A. Knopf, 1984), 152-158; John C. Poppeliers, S. Allen Chambers, Jr., and Nancy B. Schwartz, *What Style is it? A Guide to American Architecture* (Washington, D.C.: The Preservation Press, 1983), 30-31.

20. Samuel Wilson, Jr. *The Vieux Carre, New Orleans, Its Plan, Its Growth, Its Architecture* (The City of New Orleans, Louisiana, 1968), 113.

21. John G. Clark, *New Orleans, 1718-1812: An Economic History* (Baton Rouge: Louisiana State University Press, 1970), 275-76.

22. John M. Vlach, "The Shotgun House: An African Architectural Legacy," in *Common Places: Readings in American Vernacular Architecture*, Dell Upton and John M. Vlach, eds. (Athens: University of Georgia Press, 1986), 63.

23. Ibid, 67. Also see Richard Campanella, *Geographies of New Orleans: Urban Fabrics Before the Storm* (Lafayette: Center for Louisiana Studies, University of Louisiana, 2006), 127-32.

24. Fred B. Kniffen, "The Physiognomy of Rural Louisiana," *Louisiana History* 4 (1963): 293.

25. Vlach, "The Shotgun House," 63.

26. Ibid, 63.

6. The Upland South Comes to Louisiana

1. Terry G. Jordan-Bychkov, *The Upland South: The Making of an American Folk Region and Landscape* (Staunton, VA: Center for American Places, 2003).
2. Milton B. Newton, Jr., *Louisiana: A Geographical Portrait* (Baton Rouge: Geoforensics, 1987), 141-42.
3. Terry G. Jordan, "Vegetational Perception and Choice of Settlement Site in Frontier Texas," in *Pattern and Process: Research in Historical Geography*, Ralph E. Ehrenberg, ed. (Washington, D.C.: Howard University Press, 1975), 244-57.
4. Frank L. Owsley, *Plain Folk of the Old South* (Baton Rouge: Louisiana State University Press, 1949), 53.
5. Ibid, 1-2.
6. Milton B. Newton, Jr., "Of Sand Hillers, Crackers, and Cedar Choppers: The Upland South in Southern Cultures," Paper in the author's possession, n.d., 1-2.
7. Mark T. Swanson, *El Camino Real and the Great Migration Route: An Examination of 18th and 19th Century Roads in Louisiana* (New World Research, Inc., 1981), 16-17.
8. Elton M. Scott, "The Geography of Settlement in a Portion of the Texas-Louisiana Coastal Plain" (Ph.D. diss., University of Wisconsin, 1942).
9. Juan V. Haggard, "The Neutral Ground Between Louisiana and Texas," *Louisiana Historical Quarterly* 28 (1943): 1001-28.
10. Fred B. Kniffen, Hiram F. Gregory, and George A. Stokes, *The Historic Indian Tribes of Louisiana* (Baton Rouge: Louisiana State University Press, 1987), 76.
11. Louisiana Writers Project, *Louisiana: A Guide to the State* (New York: Hastings House, 1941), 46.
12. Danny Allen, "A Study of Landscape Changes in Ouachita Parish, Louisiana" (Ph.D. diss., Oklahoma State University, 1974); J. Fair Hardin, *Northeastern Louisiana: A History of the Watershed of the Red River, 1714-1937* (Shreveport: The Historical Record Association, 1937); Frederick Williamson and Lillian H. Williamson, *Northeast Louisiana: A Narrative History*

of the Ouachita River Valley and the Concordia Country (Monroe: The Historical Record Association, 1939).

13. Milton B. Newton, Jr., "The Peasant Farm of St. Helena Parish, Louisiana: A Cultural Geography" (Ph.D. diss., Louisiana State University, 1967), 6.

14. Terry G. Jordan, "The Texan Appalachia," *Annals of the Association of American Geographers* 60 (1970): 420; Fred B. Kniffen and Henry Glassie, "Building in Wood in the Eastern United States: A Time Place Perspective," *Geographical Review* 56 (1966): 65. Also see Terry G. Jordan, *Texas Log Buildings: A Folk Architecture* (Austin: University of Texas Press, 1978).

15. Jay D. Edwards, *Louisiana's Remarkable French Vernacular Architecture, 1700-1900* (Baton Rouge: Geoscience Publications, Department of Geography & Anthropology, Louisiana State University, 1988), 5-7.

16. Fred B. Kniffen, "Folk Housing: Key to Diffusion," *Annals of the Association of American Geographers* 55 (1965): 549-77.

17. Milton B.Newton, Jr. and Linda Pulliam-DeNapoli, "Log Houses as Public Occasions: A Historical Theory," *Annals of the Association of American Geographers* 67 (1977): 369-70.

18. Milton B. Newton, Jr., "Louisiana House Types: A Field Guide," (*Melanges* No. 2. Baton Rouge: Geoscience Publications, Department of Geography & Anthropology, Louisiana State University, 1971), 18.

19. Henry Glassie, *Pattern of Material Folk Culture of the Eastern United States* (Philadelphia: University of Pennsylvania Press, 1969), 94-95.

20. Milton B. Newton, Jr., "Louisiana Folk Houses," in *Louisiana Folklife: A Guide to the State*, Nicholas R. Spitzer, ed. (Baton Rouge: Louisiana Department of Culture, Recreation, and Tourism, 1985), 184.

21. Milton B. Newton, Jr., *Louisiana: A Geographical Portrait* (Baton Rouge: Geoforensics, 1987), 186.

7. The Golden Age of the Plantation

1. Sam B. Hilliard, *Atlas of Antebellum Southern Agriculture* (Baton Rouge: Louisiana State University Press, 1984), 77; Roger W. Shugg, *Origins of Class Struggle in Louisiana* (Baton Rouge: Louisiana State University Press, 1939), 4.
2. Hilliard, *Atlas of Antebellum Southern Agriculture*, 70.
3. Ibid, 70.
4. Carl A. Brasseaux and Keith P. Fontenot, *Steamboats on Louisiana's Bayous: A History and Directory* (Baton Rouge: Louisiana State University Press, 2004). For comparison, see John A. Johnson, "Pre-Steamboat Navigation on the Louisiana Mississippi River" (Ph.D. diss., Louisiana State University, 1963).
5. Joe G. Taylor, *Louisiana: A Bicentennial History* (New York: W.W. Norton, 1976), 69.
6. John D. Winters, "The Ouachita-Black," in *The Rivers and Bayous of Louisiana*, Edwin A. Davis, ed. (Baton Rouge: Louisiana Education Research Association, 1968), 26.
7. Fred B. Kniffen and Sam B. Hilliard, *Louisiana: Its Land and People* (Baton Rouge: Louisiana State University Press, 1988), 138.
8. Taylor, *Louisiana: A Bicentennial History*, 76.
9. Yvonne, Phillips, "Settlement Succession in the Tensas Basin" (Ph.D. diss., Louisiana State University, 1953).
10. By way of comparison, a well-populated area appears block-like in south-central Louisiana between the thirty-first parallel and the Gulf, with all the parishes except one having populations between ten and fifteen thousand. This block of eleven parishes, anchored by West Feliciana in the north, St. Mary in the south, St. Martin in the west, and Ascension in the east, and including East Baton Rouge Parish, had an 1830 population of 71,732. In 1850, the population had increased to 126,463. Had this area experienced the same rate of population increase as Concordia Parish, it would have had an 1850 population of 393,091! Instead, the actual increase was only 1.76 times the 1830 population.

11. Shugg, *Origins of Class Struggle in Louisiana*, 39.
12. Milton B. Newton, Jr., "Louisiana House Types: A Field Guide," (*Melanges* No. 2. Baton Rouge: Geoscience Publications, Department of Geography & Anthropology, Louisiana State University, 1971), 10.
13. David K. Gleason, *Plantation Homes of Louisiana and the Natchez Area* (Baton Rouge: Louisiana State University Press, 1982), 89; Milton B. Newton, Jr., *Louisiana: A Geographical Portrait* (Baton Rouge: Geoforensics, 1987), 188.
14. Gleason, *Plantation Homes of Louisiana and the Natchez Area*, 33.
15. Wilbur Zelinsky, "Classical Town Names: The Historical Geography of an American Idea," *Geographical Review* 57 (1967): 463-95.
16. John C. Poppeliers, S. Allen Chambers, Jr., and Nancy B. Schwartz, *What Style is it? A Guide to American Architecture* (Washington, D.C.: The Preservation Press, 1983), 36.
17. John J.G. Blumenson, *Identifying American Architecture: A Pictorial Guide to Styles and Terms, 1600-1945* (Lanham, MD: AltaMira Press, 1981), 30-31.
18. Grace Episcopal Church in West Feliciana Parish is an excellent example.
19. Wayne Andrews, *American Gothic: Its Origins, Its Trials, Its Tribulations* (New York: Random House, 1975), 107; Calder Loth and Julius T. Sadler, Jr., *The Only Proper Style: Gothic Architecture in America* (Boston: New York Graphic Society, 1975), 85-86.
20. Mark Twain, *Life on the Mississippi* (New York: Houghton, 1874), 332-33.
21. Frances Parkinson Keyes, *Steamboat Gothic* (New York: Julian Messner, 1952).

8. The Civil War and Reconstruction

1. Edwin A. Davis, *Louisiana: A Narrative History* (Baton Rouge: Claitor's Press, 1971), 243.

2. There are many names for the four-year conflict between North and South. Although "War Between the States" is less politically charged, this book follows the generally accepted term "Civil War."
3. Hodding Carter, *The Angry Scar: The Story of Reconstruction* (Garden City, New York: Doubleday, 1959); Joe G. Taylor, *Louisiana Reconstructed, 1863-1877* (Baton Rouge: Louisiana State University Press, 1974).
4. Joe G. Taylor, *Louisiana: A Bicentennial History* (New York: W.W. Norton, 1976), 87.
5. Samuel H. Lockett, *Louisiana As It Is: A Geographical and Topographical Description of the State*, Lauren C. Post, ed. (Baton Rouge: Louisiana State University Press, 1969), 22.
6. Ibid, 26.
7. Milton B. Newton, Jr., "The Peasant Farm of St. Helena Parish, Louisiana: A Cultural Geography" (Ph.D. diss., Louisiana State University, 1967).
8. Taylor, *Louisiana Reconstructed*, 6.
9. Ibid, 424.
10. Edwin A. Davis, *Louisiana: A Narrative History* (Baton Rouge: Claitor's Press, 1971), 253.
11. Milton B. Newton, Jr., "The Comprehensive Plan for St. Helena Parish, Louisiana, Historic Preservation Study, Vol. 1" (Report on file with the Louisiana Division of Historic Preservation, Baton Rouge, 1981), 32.
12. Roger W. Shugg, *Origins of Class Struggle in Louisiana* (Baton Rouge: Louisiana State University Press, 1939), 236. Also see Floyd M. Clay, "Economic Survival of the Plantation System within the Feliciana Parishes, 1865-1880" (M.A. thesis, Louisiana State University, 1962); Roger W. Shugg, "Survival of the Plantation System in Louisiana," *Journal of Southern History* 3 (1937): 311-25.
13. The actual population of the state in 1870 was 726,915.
14. They were, in descending order, New Orleans (191,949), Baton Rouge (6,498), Shreveport (4,607), Monroe (1,949), Thibodeaux (1,922), Donaldsonville (1,573), Opelousas (1,546), New Iberia

(1,472), Plaquemine (1,460), Natchitoches (1,401), Alexandria (1,218), and St. Martinville (1,190).

15. Harnett T. Kane, *Natchez on the Mississippi* (New York: Bonanza Books, 1957), 334.
16. Samuel Wilson, Jr., *The Vieux Carre, New Orleans, Its Plan, Its Growth, Its Architecture* (The City of New Orleans, Louisiana, 1968), 125.
17. Peirce F. Lewis, *New Orleans: The Making of an Urban Landscape* (Cambridge, MA: Ballinger, 1976), 61.
18. Ibid, 48.
19. Virginia McAlester and Lee McAlester, *A Field Guide to American Houses* (New York: Alfred A. Knopf, 1984), 200.
20. John C. Poppeliers, S. Allen Chambers, Jr., and Nancy B. Schwartz, *What Style is it? A Guide to American Architecture* (Washington, D.C.: The Preservation Press, 1983), 50.
21. Wilson, *The Vieux Carre*, 122.

9. The Railroad and Lumber Boom

1. R.S. Cotterill, "Beginning of Railroads in the Southwest," *Mississippi Valley Historical Review* 8 (1922): 318-26.
2. Samuel H. Lockett, *Louisiana As It Is: A Geographical and Topographical Description of the State*, Lauren C. Post, ed. (Baton Rouge: Louisiana State University Press, 1969), 132.
3. John S. Kyser, "The Evolution of Louisiana Parishes in Relation to Population Growth and Movements" (Ph.D. diss., Louisiana State University, 1938), 161.
4. Lockett, *Louisiana As It Is*, 132-33.
5. George F. Cram, *Railroad and County Map of Louisiana* (Chicago: George F. Cram, 1892).
6. Jack D.L. Holmes, "Louisiana Trees and Their Uses: Colonial Period," *Louisiana Studies* 8 (1969): 36-67; John Landreth, *The Journal of John Landreth, Surveyor: An Expedition to the Gulf Coast November 15, 1818 – May 19, 1819*, Milton B. Newton, Jr., ed. (Baton Rouge: Geoscience Publications, Department of Geography & Anthropology, Louisiana State University, 1985). The latter is an especially useful primary source because

Landreth, along with James L. Cathcart and James Hutton, was specifically looking for live oak and red cedar near Louisiana's Gulf Coast for the U.S. Navy. Newton's introduction to this LSU printing of Landreth's journal is particularly instructive.

7. A number of people have used the term "industrial lumbering" including John M. Caldwell, "The Forest of Vintage: A Geography of Industrial Lumbering in North Central Louisiana, 1890-1920" (M.A. thesis, University of Oklahoma, 1975); Nolle W. Hickman, "The Yellow Pine Industries in St. Tammany, Tangipahoa, and Washington Parishes, 1840-1915," *Louisiana Studies* 5 (1966): 75-88; Fred B. Kniffen and Sam B. Hilliard, *Louisiana: Its Land and People* (Baton Rouge: Louisiana State University Press, 1988), 166; Ervin Mancil, "Some Historical and Geographical Notes on the Cypress Lumbering Industry in Louisiana," *Louisiana Studies* 8 (1969): 14-25, and "An Historical Geography of Industrial Cypress Lumbering in Louisiana" (Ph.D. diss., Louisiana State University, 1972); George Stokes, "Lumbering in Southwest Louisiana: A Study of the Industry as a Culturo-Geographic Factor" (Ph.D. diss., Louisiana State University, 1954), "Lumbering and Western Louisiana Cultural Landscapes," *Annals of the Association of American Geographers* 47 (1957): 250-66, and "Landscape Forms and Patterns of French Origin in the Natchitoches Parish, Louisiana Area," *Louisiana Studies* 3 (1964)): 105-16.

8. George Stokes, "Lumbering in Southwest Louisiana: A Study of the Industry as a Culturo-Geographic Factor" (Ph.D. diss., Louisiana State University, 1954), 25.

9. Samuel H. Lockett, *Louisiana As It Is: A Geographical and Topographical Description of the State*, Lauren C. Post, ed. (Baton Rouge: Louisiana State University Press, 1969), 133-34.

10. George Stokes, "Lumbering in Southwest Louisiana: A Study of the Industry as a Culturo-Geographic Factor" (Ph.D. diss., Louisiana State University, 1954), 35.

11. Nolle W. Hickman, "The Yellow Pine Industries in St. Tammany, Tangipahoa, and Washington Parishes, 1840-1915," *Louisiana Studies* 5 (1966): 79.

12. Edwin A. Davis, *Louisiana: A Narrative History* (Baton Rouge: Claitor's Press, 1971), 298.

13. Fred B. Kniffen and Sam B. Hilliard, *Louisiana: Its Land and People* (Baton Rouge: Louisiana State University Press, 1988), 169.

14. John M. Caldwell, "The Forest of Vintage: A Geography of Industrial Lumbering in North Central Louisiana, 1890-1920" (M.A. thesis, University of Oklahoma, 1975), 72.

15. Fred B. Kniffen and Sam B. Hilliard, *Louisiana: Its Land and People* (Baton Rouge: Louisiana State University Press, 1988), 169.

16. George Stokes, "Lumbering in Southwest Louisiana: A Study of the Industry as a Culturo-Geographic Factor" (Ph.D. diss., Louisiana State University, 1954), 35.

17. Fred B. Kniffen, "Material Culture in the Geographic Interpretation of the Landscape," in *The Human Mirror: Material and Spatial Images of Man*, Miles Richardson, ed. (Baton Rouge: Louisiana State University Press, 1974), 260; William H. Perrin, ed. *Southwest Louisiana: Biographical and Historical* (New Orleans: Gulf Publishing Company, 1891).

18. Fred B. Kniffen, "The Physiognomy of Rural Louisiana," *Louisiana History* 4 (1963): 297.

19. Milton B. Newton, Jr., *Louisiana: A Geographical Portrait* (Baton Rouge: Geoforensics, 1987), 149.

20. Edwin A. Davis, *Louisiana: A Narrative History* (Baton Rouge: Claitor's Press, 1971), 295.

21. Lauren C. Post, *Cajun Sketches from the Prairies of Southwest Louisiana* (Baton Rouge: Louisiana State University Press, 1974), 79.

22. Milton B. Newton, Jr., *Louisiana: A Geographical Portrait* (Baton Rouge: Geoforensics, 1987), 151.

23. Virginia McAlester and Lee McAlester, *A Field Guide to American Houses* (New York: Alfred A. Knopf, 1984), 63.

24. Milton B. Newton, Jr., *Louisiana: A Geographical Portrait* (Baton Rouge: Geoforensics, 1987), 153.

25. Fred B. Kniffen, "The Physiognomy of Rural Louisiana," *Louisiana History* 4 (1963): 293, and "Material Culture in the

Geographic Interpretation of the Landscape," in *The Human Mirror: Material and Spatial Images of Man*, Miles Richardson, ed. (Baton Rouge: Louisiana State University Press, 1974), 261.

26. John M. Vlach, "The Shotgun House: An African Architectural Legacy," in *Common Places: Readings in American Vernacular Architecture*, Dell Upton and John M. Vlach eds. (Athens: University of Georgia Press, 1986), 61; Milton B. Newton, Jr., "Louisiana Folk Houses," in *Louisiana Folklife: A Guide to the State*, Nicholas R. Spitzer, ed. Baton Rouge: Louisiana Department of Culture, Recreation, and Tourism, 1985), 186.

27. Kniffen, "The Physiognomy of Rural Louisiana," 295.

28. McAlester and McAlester, *A Field Guide to American Houses*, 100-101.

29. Milton B. Newton, Jr., "Louisiana House Types: A Field Guide," *Melanges* No. 2 (Baton Rouge: Geoscience Publications, Department of Geography & Anthropology, Louisiana State University, 1971), 16.

30. McAlester and McAlester, *A Field Guide to American Houses*, 268.

10. Historic Preservation in the Bayou State

1. The preservation community in this country consists of a partnership between avocational and professional participants within the context of governmental, academic, organizational, and corporate involvement. Although the literature of historic preservation is sizable, the following sources should offer a small sense of this participation at the local, state, and national levels, as well as the range of cultural resources considered. Arnold R. Alanen and Robert Z. Melnick, eds., *Preserving Cultural Landscapes in America* (Baltimore: Johns Hopkins University Press, 2000); Nancy W. Hawkins, *Preserving Louisiana's Legacy: Everyone Can Help* (Baton Rouge: Louisiana Division of Archaeology, Anthropological Study No. 5, 1982); Peter B. Mires, "Teaching Geographic Field Methods to Cultural Resource Management Technicians," *Journal of Geography* 103

(2004): 8-15. In addition, *Preservation* magazine, published by the National Trust for Historic Preservation, is an excellent resource for anyone interested in this topic.

2. Peter B. Mires, "Relationships of Louisiana Colonial Land Claims with Potential Natural Vegetation and Historic Standing Structures: A GIS Approach," *The Professional Geographer* 45 (1993): 342-50. The sample size consisted of 557 individually listed historic houses on the National Register of Historic Places on file with the Louisiana Division of Historic Preservation, as well as structures from a survey of Louisiana vernacular architecture conducted by Dr. Jay D. Edwards of Louisiana State University.

3. Peter B. Mires, "Predicting the Past: The Geography of Settlement in Louisiana, 1699-1890, and its Application to Historic Preservation" (Ph.D. diss., Louisiana State University, 1988), 229-233.

4. W.J. Cash, *The Mind of the South* (New York: Alfred A. Knopf, 1941), ix. Donna Fricker says much the same thing in "The Gothic Revival Style," in *Louisiana Architecture: A Handbook on Styles*, by Jonathan Fricker, Donna Fricker, and Patricia L. Duncan (Lafayette: Center for Louisiana Studies, University of Louisiana, 1998), 18. It has been noted elsewhere that in Louisiana the Greek Revival style is jokingly referred to as "Greek Survival" because it lingered here long after the period of national popularity.

5. The National Register criteria for evaluation were initially published in the *Code of Federal Regulations, Title 36, Part 60* in 1976. For more on the mechanics of historic preservation see the dated, but still useful, Thomas F. King, Patricia Parker Hickman, and Gary Berg, *Anthropology in Historic Preservation: Caring for Culture's Clutter* (New York: Academic Press, 1977).

6. Donald W. Meinig, ed., *Interpretation of Ordinary Landscapes: Geographical Essays* (New York: Oxford University Press, 1979).

7. James Conaway, *Vanishing America: In Pursuit of our Elusive Landscapes* (Emeryville, CA: Shoemaker Hoard, 2007).

Bibliography

Alanen, Arnold R. and Robert Z. Melnick, eds. *Preserving Cultural Landscapes in America*. Baltimore: Johns Hopkins University Press, 2000.

Albrecht, Andrew C. "The Origin and Early Settlement of Baton Rouge, Louisiana." *Louisiana Historical Quarterly* 28 (1945): 5-68.

Allen, Danny. "A Study of Landscape Changes in Ouachita Parish, Louisiana." Ph.D. dissertation, Oklahoma State University, 1974.

Andrews, Wayne. *American Gothic: Its Origins, Its Trials, Its Tribulations*. New York: Random House, 1975.

Bennett, Cheryl A. "The Creation of Tangipahoa Parish—1869." *Papers of the Southeast Louisiana Historical Association* 1 (1974): 58-63.

Bjork, David K. "Documents Relating to Alexandro O'Reilly and an Expedition sent out by him from New Orleans to Natchitoches, 1769-1770." *Louisiana Historical Quarterly* 7 (1924): 20-39.

Blumenson, John J.G. *Identifying American Architecture: A Pictorial Guide to Styles and Terms, 1600-1945*. Lanham, MD: AltaMira Press, 1981.

Bolton, Herbert E. *The Spanish Borderlands*. New Haven, CT: Yale University Press, 1921.

Brasseaux, Carl A. *The Founding of New Acadia: The Beginnings of Acadian Life in Louisiana, 1765-1803*. Baton Rouge: Louisiana State University Press, 1987.

Brasseaux, Carl A. and Keith P. Fontenot. *Steamboats on Louisiana's Bayous: A History and Directory*. Baton Rouge: Louisiana State University Press, 2004.

Bridges, Katherine and Winston De Ville. "Natchitoches in 1766." *Louisiana History* 4 (1963): 145-59.

Broek, Jan O.M. *The Santa Clara Valley, California: A Study in Landscape Changes*. Utrecht, The Netherlands: Utrecht University, 1932.

_____. *Geography: Its Scope and Spirit*. Columbus, OH: Charles E. Merrill, 1965.

Brown, Clair. *Louisiana Trees and Shrubs*. Baton Rouge: Louisiana Commission of Forestry, 1945.

Brown, Ralph H. *Mirror for Americans: Likeness of the Eastern Seaboard, 1810*. New York: American Geographical Society, 1943.

_____. *Historical Geography of the United States*. New York: Harcourt, Brace, 1948.

Brutin, Ignace Francois. *Plan du Fort des Natcheitoches*. Paris: Archives Nationales, 1733.

Caldwell, Joan G. "Italianate Domestic Architecture in New Orleans, 1850-1880." Ph.D. dissertation, Tulane University, 1975.

Caldwell, John M. "The Forest of Vintage: A Geography of Industrial Lumbering in North Central Louisiana, 1890-1920." M.A. thesis, University of Oklahoma, 1975.

Campanella, Richard. *Geographies of New Orleans: Urban Fabrics Before the Storm*. Lafayette: Center for Louisiana Studies, University of Louisiana, 2006.

Carter, Clarence E. "The Beginnings of British West Florida." *Mississippi Valley Historical Review* 4 (1917): 314-41.

Carter, Hodding. *The Angry Scar: The Story of Reconstruction*. Garden City, NY: Doubleday, 1959.

Cash, W.J. *The Mind of the South*. New York: Alfred A. Knopf, 1941.

Chabreck, Robert H. and Greg Linscombe. *Vegetative Type Map of the Louisiana Coastal Marshes*. New Orleans: Louisiana Department of Wildlife and Fisheries, 1978.

Clark, Andrew H. "Historical Geography." In *American Geography: Inventory and Prospect*, ed. Preston E. James and Clarence F. Jones, pp. 70-105. Syracuse, NY: Syracuse University Press, 1954.

Clark, John G. *New Orleans, 1718-1812: An Economic History*. Baton Rouge: Louisiana State University Press, 1970.

Clay, Floyd M. "Economic Survival of the Plantation System within the Feliciana Parishes, 1865-1880." M.A. thesis, Louisiana State University, 1962.

Colten, Craig E., ed. *Transforming New Orleans and its Environs: Centuries of Change*. Pittsburgh: University of Pittsburgh Press, 2001.

Comeaux, Malcolm L. "Settlement and Folk Occupations of the Atchafalaya Basin." Ph.D. dissertation, Louisiana State University, 1969.

_____. *Atchafalaya Swamp Life*. Baton Rouge: Geoscience Publications, Department of Geography & Anthropology, Louisiana State University, 1972.

Conaway, James. *Vanishing America: In Pursuit of our Elusive Landscapes*. Emeryville, CA: Shoemaker Hoard, 2007.

Codrescu, Andrei. *New Orleans, Mon Amour: Twenty Years of Writings from the City*. Chapel Hill, NC: Algonquin Books, 2006.

Cotterill, R.S. "Beginning of Railroads in the Southwest." *Mississippi Valley Historical Review* 8 (1922): 318-26.

Cram, George F. *Railroad and County Map of Louisiana*. Chicago: George F. Cram, 1892.

Darby, William. A Geographical Description of the State of Louisiana. Philadelphia: J. Melish, 1816.

Daspit, Fred. *Louisiana Architecture: 1714-1820*. Lafayette: Center for Louisiana Studies, University of Louisiana, 2005.

_____. *Louisiana Architecture: 1820-1840*. Lafayette: Center for Louisiana Studies, University of Louisiana, 2005.

_____. *Louisiana Architecture: 1840-1860*. Lafayette: Center for Louisiana Studies, University of Louisiana, 2007.

Davis, Edwin A., ed. *The Rivers and Bayous of Louisiana*. Baton Rouge: Louisiana Education Research Association, 1968.

_____. *Louisiana: A Narrative History*. 3rd ed. Baton Rouge: Claitor's Press, 1971.

Deetz, James F. *Invitation to Archaeology*. New York: Natural History Press, 1967.

DeHart, Jess. *Louisiana's Historic Towns*. New Orleans: Hamlet House, 1983.

Deiler, J. Hanno. *The Settlement of the German Coast of Louisiana and the Creoles of German Descent*. Philadelphia: Americana-Germanica Press, 1909.

De' L'Isle, Guillaume. *Carte de la Louisiane et du Cours du Mississippi*. Paris: Guillaume De L'Isle, 1734.

De Ville, Winston. "The Opelousas Post, From the Earliest Settlement to 1803." M.A. thesis, Louisiana State University, 1963.

_____. "Rapides Post on the Red River: Census and Military Documents for Central Louisiana, 1769-1800." Ville Platte, LA: Privately printed, 1985.

Ditchy, Jay K. "Early Census Tables of Louisiana." *Louisiana Historical Quarterly* 13 (1930): 205-29.

Edwards, Jay D. "Cultural Syncretism in the Louisiana Creole Cottage." *Louisiana Folklore Miscellany* 4 (1980): 9-40.

_____. *A Survey of Louisiana French Vernacular Architecture*. Baton Rouge: Louisiana State University, Museum of Geoscience, 1982.

_____. "French." In *America's Architectural Roots: Ethnic Groups that Built America*, ed. Dell Upton, pp. 62-67. Washington, D.C.: National Trust for Historic Preservation, 1986.

_____. *Louisiana's Remarkable French Vernacular Architecture, 1700-1900*. Baton Rouge: Geoscience Publications, Department of Geography & Anthropology, Louisiana State University, 1988.

Edwards, Jay D. and Nicolas Kariouk. *A Creole Lexicon: Architecture, Landscape, People*. Baton Rouge: Louisiana State University Press, 2004.

Edwards, Jay D. and Tom Wells. *Historic Louisiana Nails: Aids to the Dating of Old Buildings*. Baton Rouge: Geoscience Publications, Department of Geography & Anthropology, Louisiana State University, 1994.

Estaville, Lawrence E. "The Louisiana French Culture Region: Geographic Morphologies in the Nineteenth Century." Ph.D. dissertation, University of Oklahoma, 1984.

Farnsworth, Jean M. and Ann M. Masson, eds. *The Architecture of Colonial Louisiana: Collected Essays of Samuel Wilson, Jr.* Lafayette: Center for Louisiana Studies, University of Louisiana, 1987.

Ford, James A. "The Type Concept Revisited." *American Anthropologist* 56 (1954): 42-54.

Fricker, Jonathan. "The Origins of the Creole Raised Plantation House." *Louisiana History* 25 (1984): 137-53.

Fricker, Jonathan, Donna Fricker, and Patricia L. Duncan. *Louisiana Architecture: A Handbook on Styles*. Lafayette: Center for Louisiana Studies, University of Louisiana, 1998.

Giraud, Marcel. *A History of French Louisiana. Volume 1, The Reign of Louis XIV, 1698-1715*. Baton Rouge: Louisiana State University Press, 1953.

Glassie, Henry. *Pattern of Material Folk Culture of the Eastern United States*. Philadelphia: University of Pennsylvania Press, 1969.

Gleason, David K. *Plantation Homes of Louisiana and the Natchez Area*. Baton Rouge: Louisiana State University Press, 1982.

Gomez, Gay. *A Wetland Biography: Seasons on Louisiana's Chenier Plain*. Austin: University of Texas Press, 1998.

Graebner, Norman A, Gilbert C. Fite, and Philip L. White. *A History of the American People*. New York: McGraw Hill, 1971.

Haggard, Juan V. "The Neutral Ground Between Louisiana and Texas." *Louisiana Historical Quarterly* 28 (1943): 1001-28.

Hardin, J. Fair. *Northeastern Louisiana: A History of the Watershed of the Red River, 1714-1937*. Shreveport: The Historical Record Association, 1937.

Harris, Richard C. *The Seigneurial System in Early Canada*. Madison: University of Wisconsin Press, 1966.

Hartshorne, Richard. *The Nature of Geography*. Lancaster, PA: Association of American Geographers, 1949.

Hawkins, Nancy W. *Preserving Louisiana's Legacy: Everyone Can Help*. Baton Rouge: Louisiana Division of Archaeology, Anthropological Study No. 5, 1982.

Heck, Robert W. "Building Traditions in the Acadian Parishes." In *The Cajuns: Essays on Their History and Culture*, ed. Glenn R. Conrad, pp. 161-72. Lafayette: University of Southwestern Louisiana, 1978.

Hickman, Nollie W. "The Yellow Pine Industries in St. Tammany, Tangipahoa, and Washington Parishes, 1840-1915." *Louisiana Studies* 5 (1966): 75-88.

Hilliard, Sam B. *Atlas of Antebellum Southern Agriculture*. Baton Rouge: Louisiana State University Press, 1984.

Holmes, Jack D.L. "Louisiana Trees and Their Uses: Colonial Period." *Louisiana Studies* 8 (1969): 36-67.

Howard, Clinton N. *The British Development of West Florida, 1763-1769*. Berkeley: University of California Press, 1947.

Hudson, Charles. *The Southeastern Indians*. Knoxville: University of Tennessee Press, 1976.

Jacobs, Harry. *Natural Vegetation Map of Louisiana*. Baton Rouge: Louisiana State Board of Engineers, 1937.

Johnson, Cecil. *British West Florida, 1763-1783*. New Haven, CT: Yale University Press, 1943.

Johnson, John A. "Pre-Steamboat Navigation on the Louisiana Mississippi River." Ph.D. dissertation, Louisiana State University, 1963.

Jones, Terry L. *The Louisiana Journey*. Layton, UT: Gibbs Smith, 2007.

Jordan, Terry G. "Between the Forest and the Prairie." *Agricultural History* 38 (1964): 205-16.

_____. "The Texan Appalachia." *Annals of the Association of American Geographers* 60 (1970): 409-27.

_____. "Vegetational Perception and Choice of Settlement Site in Frontier Texas." In *Pattern and Process: Research in Historical Geography*, ed. Ralph E. Ehrenberg, pp. 244-57. Washington, D.C.: Howard University Press, 1975.

_____. *Texas Log Buildings: A Folk Architecture*. Austin: University of Texas Press, 1978.

Jordan, Terry G. and Matti Kaups. *The American Backwoods Frontier: An Ethnic and Ecological Interpretation*. Baltimore: Johns Hopkins University Press, 1992.

Jordan-Bychkov, Terry G. *The Upland South: The Making of an American Folk Region and Landscape*. Staunton, VA: Center for American Places, 2003.

Kane, Harnett T. *The Bayous of Louisiana*. New York: William Morrow, 1943.

_____. *Deep Delta Country*. New York: Duell, Sloan & Pearce, 1944.

_____. *Natchez on the Mississippi*. New York: Bonanza Books, 1957.

Kennedy, J. Gerald. *The Astonished Traveler: William Darby, Frontier Geographer and Man of Letters*. Baton Rouge: Louisiana State University Press, 1981.

Keyes, Frances Parkinson. *Steamboat Gothic*. New York: Julian Messner, 1952.

King, Ameda R. "Social and Economic Life in Spanish Louisiana, 1763-1783." Ph.D. dissertation, University of Illinois, Urbana-Champaign, 1931.

King, Thomas F., Patricia Parker Hickman, and Gary Berg. *Anthropology in Historic Preservation: Caring for Culture's Clutter*. New York: Academic Press, 1977.

Kniffen, Fred B. "Louisiana House Types." *Annals of the Association of American Geographers* 26 (1936): 179-93.

_____. "Geography and the Past." *Journal of Geography* 50 (1951): 126-29.

_____. "Wither Cultural Geography?" *Annals of the Association of American Geographers* 44 (1954): 222-23.

_____. "The Physiognomy of Rural Louisiana." *Louisiana History* 4 (1963): 291-99.

_____. "Folk Housing: Key to Diffusion." *Annals of the Association of American Geographers* 55 (1965): 549-77.

_____. "Why Folk Housing?" *Annals of the Association of American Geographers* 69 (1979): 59-63.

_____. "Material Culture in the Geographic Interpretation of the Landscape." In *The Human Mirror: Material and Spatial Images of Man*, ed. Miles Richardson, pp. 252-268. Baton Rouge: Louisiana State University Press, 1974.

Kniffen, Fred B. and Henry Glassie. "Building in Wood in the Eastern United States: A Time Place Perspective." *Geographical Review* 56 (1966): 40-66.

Kniffen, Fred B., Hiram F. Gregory, and George A. Stokes. *The Historic Indian Tribes of Louisiana*. Baton Rouge: Louisiana State University Press, 1987.

Kniffen, Fred B. and Sam B. Hilliard. *Louisiana: Its Land and People*. Revised ed. Baton Rouge: Louisiana State University Press, 1988.

Knipmeyer, William B. "Settlement Succession in Eastern French Louisiana." Ph.D. dissertation, Louisiana State University, 1956.

Kuchler, A.W. *Potential Natural Vegetation of the Coterminious United States*. American Geographical Society, Special Publication No. 36, 1964.

Kyser, John S. "The Evolution of Louisiana Parishes in Relation to Population Growth and Movements." Ph.D. dissertation, Louisiana State University, 1938.

Lafon, Bernard. *Carte Generale du Territoire d'Oreleans*. New Orleans: Bernard Lafon, 1806.

Landreth, John. *The Journal of John Landreth, Surveyor: An Expedition to the Gulf Coast November 15, 1818 – May 19, 1819*, ed. Milton B. Newton, Jr. Baton Rouge: Geoscience Publications, Department of Geography & Anthropology, Louisiana State University, 1985.

Langness, Lewis L. *The Study of Culture*. 3rd ed. Novato, CA: Chandler & Sharp, 2005.

Lebreton, Marietta M. "History of the Territory of Orleans, 1803-1812." Ph.D. dissertation, Louisiana State University, 1969.

Legan, Marshall S. "Railroad Sentiment in North Louisiana in the 1850's." *Louisiana History* 17 (1976): 125-42.

LePage du Pratz, Antoine S. *The History of Louisiana*. A facsimile reproduction of the 1774 book, ed. Joseph G. Tregle, Jr. Baton Rouge: Louisiana State University Press, 1975.

Lewis, John C. "The Settlement Succession of the Boeuf River Basin, Louisiana." Ph.D. dissertation, Louisiana State University, 1973.

Lewis, Peirce F. *New Orleans: The Making of an Urban Landscape*. Cambridge, MA: Ballinger, 1976.

Lockett, Samuel H. *Louisiana As It Is: A Geographical and Topographical Description of the State*. Initial printing of the 1873 manuscript, ed. Lauren C. Post. Baton Rouge: Louisiana State University Press, 1969.

Longfellow, Henry W. *Evangeline: A Tale of Acadie*. Reprint of the 1847 original, with an introduction by C. Bruce Fergusson. Halifax, Nova Scotia: H.H. Marshall, 1976.

Loth, Calder and Julius T. Sadler, Jr. *The Only Proper Style: Gothic Architecture in America*. Boston: New York Graphic Society, 1975.

Louisiana Writers Project. *Louisiana: A Guide to the State*. New York: Hastings House, 1941.

Maass, John. *The Gingerbread Age: A View of Victorian America*. New York: Rinehart, 1957.

McAlester, Virginia and Lee McAlester. *A Field Guide to American Houses*. New York: Alfred A. Knopf, 1984.

McIntire, William G. "Methods of Correlating Cultural Remains with Stages of Coastal Development." In *Environment and Culture*, ed.

H. Jesse Walker and Milton B. Newton, Jr., pp. 117-25. Baton Rouge: Geoscience Publications, Department of Geography & Anthropology, Louisiana State University, 1978.

McKenna, John R. "The Role of Water Transportation in the Settlement of Bayou Manchac and the Amite River, Louisiana." M.A. thesis, Louisiana State University, 1975.

McPhee, John A. *The Control of Nature*. New York: Farrar, Straus, and Giroux, 1990.

Maduell, Charles R., Jr., trans. *The Census Tables for the French Colony of Louisiana from 1699 through 1732*. Baltimore: Genealogical Publishing Company, 1972.

Maloof, Joan. *Teaching the Trees: Lessons from the Forest*. Athens: University of Georgia Press, 2005.

Mancil, Ervin. "Some Historical and Geographical Notes on the Cypress Lumbering Industry in Louisiana." *Louisiana Studies* 8 (1969): 14-25.

_____. "An Historical Geography of Industrial Cypress Lumbering in Louisiana." Ph.D. dissertation, Louisiana State University, 1972.

Martin, F. Lester. *Folk and Styled Architecture in North Louisiana: The Hill Parishes*. Lafayette: University of Southwestern Louisiana, 1989.

_____. *Folk and Styled Architecture in North Louisiana: The River Parishes*. Lafayette: Center for Louisiana Studies, University of Louisiana, 2000.

Meinig, Donald W. *Imperial Texas*. Austin: University of Texas Press, 1969.

_____. *The Shaping of America, Volume I: Atlantic America, 1492-1800*. New Haven, CT: Yale University Press, 1986.

Meinig, Donald W., ed. *Interpretation of Ordinary Landscapes: Geographical Essays*. New York: Oxford University Press, 1979.

Mikesell, Marvin W. "The Rise and Decline of 'Sequent Occupance:' A Chapter in the History of American Geography." In *Geographies of the Mind*, ed. David Lowenthal and Martyn J. Bowden, pp. 149-69. New York: Oxford University Press, 1976.

Mills, Gary B. *The Forgotten People: Cane River's Creoles of Color*. Baton Rouge: Louisiana State University Press, 1977.

Mires, Peter B. "Architectural History." In *Southeast Louisiana Cultural Resource Management Plan, Appendix A: Cultural History*, ed. Kathleen Bowman and Keith Landreth, pp. 189-231. Report on file with the U.S. Army Corps of Engineers, New Orleans District, 1987.

_____. "Predicting the Past: The Geography of Settlement in Louisiana, 1699-1890, and its Application to Historic Preservation." Ph.D. dissertation, Louisiana State University, 1988.

_____. "Relationships of Louisiana Colonial Land Claims with Potential Natural Vegetation and Historic Standing Structures: A GIS Approach." *The Professional Geographer* 45 (1993): 342-50.

_____. Review of *Everyday Architecture of the Mid-Atlantic: Looking at Buildings and Landscapes*, by Gabrielle M. Lanier and Bernard L. Herman (Johns Hopkins University Press, 1997). *Historical Archaeology* 33 (1999): 134-36.

_____. "Teaching Geographic Field Methods to Cultural Resource Management Technicians." *Journal of Geography* 103 (2004): 8-15.

_____. "Of Storms and Statues: Reflections on Louisiana." *FOCUS on Geography* 51 (2008): 34-37.

Mitchell, Jennie O. and Dabney Calhoun. "The Marquis de Maison Rouge, the Baron de Bastrop and Colonel Abraham Morehouse – Three Ouachita Valley Soldiers of Fortune. The Maison Rouge and Bastrop Grants." *Louisiana Historical Quarterly* 20 (1937): 289-462.

Moore, John P. *Revolt in Louisiana: The Spanish Occupation, 1766-1770.* Baton Rouge: Louisiana State University Press, 1976.

National Trust for Historic Preservation. "Getting to Know Your Early Twentieth-Century Neighborhood." *Conserve Neighborhoods* No. 25. Washington, D.C.: National Trust for Historic Preservation, 1982.

Nardini, Louis R. *No Man's Land: A History of El Camino Real.* New Orleans: Pelican Publishing Company, 1961.

Nelson, Thomas C. and Walter M. Zillgitt. *A Forest Atlas of the South.* United States Department of Agriculture, Forest Service, Southern Forest Experiment Station, New Orleans, 1969.

Neuman, Robert W. *An Introduction to Louisiana Archaeology.* Baton Rouge: Louisiana State University Press, 1984.

Newton, Milton B., Jr. "The Peasant Farm of St. Helena Parish, Louisiana: A Cultural Geography." Ph.D. dissertation, Louisiana State University, 1967.

_____. "Route Geography and the Routes of St. Helena Parish, Louisiana." *Annals of the Association of American Geographers* 60 (1970): 134-52.

_____. "Louisiana House Types: A Field Guide." *Melanges* No. 2. Baton Rouge: Geoscience Publications, Department of Geography & Anthropology, Louisiana State University, 1971.

_____. *Atlas of Louisiana.* Baton Rouge: Geoscience Publications, Department of Geography & Anthropology, Louisiana State University, 1972.

_____. "Cultural Preadaptation and the Upland South." In "Man and Cultural Heritage," ed. H. Jesse Walker and William G. Haag, *Geoscience and Man* 5 (1974): 143-54. Baton Rouge: Geoscience Publications, Department of Geography & Anthropology, Louisiana State University, 1974.

_____. "Settlement Patterns as Artifacts of Social Structure." In *The Human Mirror: Material and Spatial Images of Man*, ed. Miles Richardson, pp. 339-361. Baton Rouge: Louisiana State University Press, 1974.

_____. "The Comprehensive Plan for St. Helena Parish, Louisiana, Historic Preservation Study, Vol. 1." Report on file with the Louisiana Division of Historic Preservation, Baton Rouge, 1981.

_____. "Louisiana Folk Houses." In *Louisiana Folklife: A Guide to the State*, ed. Nicholas R. Spitzer, pp. 179-89. Baton Rouge: Louisiana Department of Culture, Recreation, and Tourism, 1985.

_____. *Louisiana: A Geographical Portrait.* Baton Rouge: Geoforensics, 1987.

_____. "Of Sand Hillers, Crackers, and Cedar Choppers: The Upland South in Southern Cultures." Paper in the author's possession, n.d.

Newton, Milton B., Jr. and Linda Pulliam-DeNapoli. "Log Houses as Public Occasions: A Historical Theory." *Annals of the Association of American Geographers* 67 (1977): 360-83.

Newton, Milton B., Jr. and C. Nicholas Raphael. "Relic Roads of East Feliciana Parish, Louisiana." *The Geographical Review* 61 (1971): 250-64.

Noel Hume, Ivor. *Historical Archaeology.* New York: Alfred A. Knopf, 1969.

Odum, E. Dale. "The Vicksburg, Shreveport, and Texas: The Fortunes of a Scalawag Railroad." *Southwestern Social Science Quarterly* 44 (1963): 277-85.

Oszuscik, Philippe. "French Creole Housing on the Gulf Coast: The Early Years." *Pioneer America Society Transactions* 6 (1983): 49-58.

_____. "The French Creole Cottage and its Caribbean Connection." In *French and Germans in the Mississippi Valley: Landscape and Cultural Traditions*, ed. Michael Roark, pp. 61-78. Cape Girardeau,

MO: Center for Regional History and Cultural Heritage, Southeast Missouri State University, 1988.

Ostby, Otis L., III. "French Architecture in the Mississippi River Valley, 1680-1803." M.A. thesis, University of Virginia, 1981.

Owsley, Frank L. *Plain Folk of the Old South.* Baton Rouge: Louisiana State University Press, 1949.

Parkman, Francis. "The French in Louisiana, 1699-1712." Ph.D. dissertation, Harvard University, 1930.

Perrin, William H., ed. *Southwest Louisiana: Biographical and Historical.* New Orleans: Gulf Publishing Company, 1891.

Peterson, Charles E. "Early Ste. Genevieve and its Architecture." *Missouri Historical Review* 35 (1941): 223-27.

Phillips, Steven J. *Old House Dictionary: An Illustrated Guide to American Domestic Architecture (1600 to 1940).* Lakewood, CO: American Source Books, 1989.

Phillips, Yvonne. "Settlement Succession in the Tensas Basin." Ph.D. dissertation, Louisiana State University, 1953.

Pillsbury, Richard and Andrew Kardos. *A Field Guide to the Folk Architecture of the Northeastern United States.* Hanover, NH: Geography Publications at Dartmouth No. 8, 1970.

Pittman, Captain Philip. *The Present State of European Settlements on the Mississippi.* A facsimile reproduction of the 1770 book, ed. John F. McDermott. Memphis, TN: Memphis State University, 1977.

Poesch, Jessie and Barbara S. Bacot, eds. *Louisiana Buildings, 1720-1940: The Historic American Buildings Survey.* Baton Rouge: Louisiana State University Press, 1997.

Poppeliers, John C., S. Allen Chambers, Jr., and Nancy B. Schwartz. *What Style is it? A Guide to American Architecture.* Washington, D.C.: The Preservation Press, 1983.

Post, Lauren C. "Cultural Geography of the Prairies of Southwest Louisiana." Ph.D. dissertation, University of California, Berkeley, 1937.

_____. "Samuel Henry Lockett (1837-1891) – A Sketch of his Life and Work." *Louisiana History* 5 (1964): 421-41.

_____. *Cajun Sketches from the Prairies of Southwest Louisiana*. Baton Rouge: Louisiana State University Press, 1974.

Reed, Merl E. "Louisiana's Transportation Revolution: The Railroads, 1830-1850." Ph.D. dissertation, Louisiana State University, 1957.

Rehder, John B. "Sugar Plantation Settlements of South Louisiana: A Cultural Geography." Ph.D. dissertation, Louisiana State University, 1971.

_____. "Diagnostic Landscape Traits of Sugar Plantations in Southern Louisiana." In "Man and Environment in the Lower Mississippi Valley," ed. Sam B. Hilliard, *Geoscience and Man* 19 (1978): 135-50. Baton Rouge: Geoscience Publications, Department of Geography & Anthropology, Louisiana State University, 1978.

_____. *Delta Sugar: Louisiana's Vanishing Plantation Landscape*. Baltimore: Johns Hopkins University Press, 1999.

Reps, John W. *Town Planning in Frontier America*. Princeton, NJ: Princeton University Press, 1965.

Scott, Elton M. "The Geography of Settlement in a Portion of the Texas-Louisiana Coastal Plain." Ph.D. dissertation, University of Wisconsin, 1942.

Scroggs, W.O. "Early Trade and Travel in the Lower Mississippi Valley." *Proceedings of the Mississippi Valley Historical Association* 2 (1909): 1-22.

Seramuzza, V.M. "Galveztown, A Spanish Settlement of Colonial Louisiana." *Louisiana Historical Quarterly* 13 (1930): 553-609.

Shugg, Roger W. "Survival of the Plantation System in Louisiana." *Journal of Southern History* 3 (1937): 311-25.

_____. *Origins of Class Struggle in Louisiana*. Baton Rouge: Louisiana State University Press, 1939.

Skipwith, Henry. *East Feliciana, Louisiana, Past and Present: Sketches of the Pioneers*. New Orleans: Hopkins, 1892.

Spitzer, Nicholas R., ed. *Louisiana Folklife: A Guide to the State*. Louisiana Folklife Program, Baton Rouge. 1985.

Stahle, David. "Tree-Ring Dating of Historic Buildings in Arkansas." *Tree-Ring Bulletin* 39 (1979): 1-28.

Sternberg, Mary Ann. *Winding Through Time: The Forgotten History and Present-Day Peril of Bayou Manchac*. Baton Rouge: Louisiana State University Press, 2007.

Sternitzke, Herbert S. *Louisiana Forests*. United States Department of Agriculture, Forest Service, Southern Forest Experiment Station, New Orleans, 1965.

Stokes, George. "Lumbering in Southwest Louisiana: A Study of the Industry as a Culturo-Geographic Factor." Ph.D. dissertation, Louisiana State University, 1954.

_____. "Lumbering and Western Louisiana Cultural Landscapes." *Annals of the Association of American Geographers* 47 (1957): 250-66.

_____. "Landscape Forms and Patterns of French Origin in the Natchitoches Parish, Louisiana Area." *Louisiana Studies* 3 (1964): 105-16.

Swanson, Mark T. *El Camino Real and the Great Migration Route: An Examination of 18th and 19th Century Roads in Louisiana*. Report on file with the Louisiana State Historic Preservation Office, Baton Rouge, 1981.

Taylor, James W. "Louisiana Land Survey Systems." *Southwestern Social Science Quarterly* 31 (1950): 275-82.

_____. "The Agricultural Settlement Succession in the Prairies of Southwest Louisiana." Ph.D. dissertation, Louisiana State University, 1956.

Taylor, Joe G. *Louisiana Reconstructed, 1863-1877.* Baton Rouge: Louisiana State University Press, 1974.

_____. *Louisiana: A Bicentennial History.* New York: W.W. Norton, 1976.

Treat, Victor H. "Migration into Louisiana, 1834-1880." Ph.D. dissertation, University of Texas, Austin, 1967.

Twain, Mark (Samuel L. Clemens). *Life on the Mississippi.* New York: Houghton, 1874.

Upton, Dell and John M. Vlach, eds. *Common Places: Readings in American Vernacular Architecture.* Athens: University of Georgia Press, 1986.

Vlach, John M. "Sources of the Shotgun House: African and Caribbean Antecedents for Afro-American Architecture." Ph.D. dissertation, Indiana University, 1975.

_____. "The Shotgun House: An African Architectural Legacy." In *Common Places: Readings in American Vernacular Architecture,* ed. Dell Upton and John M. Vlach, pp. 58-78. Athens: University of Georgia Press, 1986.

_____. "Afro-American." In *America's Architectural Roots: Ethnic Groups that Built America,* ed. D. Upton, pp. 42-47. Washington, D.C.: The Preservation Press, 1986.

Vogt, Lloyd. *New Orleans Houses: A House-Watcher's Guide.* Gretna, LA: Pelican Publishing Company, 1985.

Voorhies, Jacqueline K., trans. *Some Late Eighteenth Century Louisianians: Census Records of the Colony, 1758-1796.* Lafayette: University of Southwestern Louisiana, 1973.

Whittlesey, Derwent. "Sequent Occupance." *Annals of the Association of American Geographers* 19 (1929): 162-65.

Whiffen, Marcus. *American Architecture Since 1780: A Guide to Styles.* Cambridge, MA: M.I.T. Press, 1969.

Willey, Gordon R. and Philip Phillips. *Method and Theory in American Archaeology.* Chicago: University of Chicago Press, 1958.

Willey, Gordon R. and Jeremy A. Sabloff. *A History of American Archaeology.* 3rd ed. San Francisco: W.H. Freeman, 1993.

Williamson, Frederick W. and Lillian H. Williamson. *Northeast Louisiana: A Narrative History of the Ouachita River Valley and the Concordia Country.* Monroe, LA: The Historical Record Association, 1939.

Wilson, Eugene M. "Folk Houses of Northern Alabama." Ph.D. dissertation, Louisiana State University, 1969.

Wilson, Samuel, Jr. *The Vieux Carre, New Orleans, Its Plan, Its Growth, Its Architecture.* The City of New Orleans, Louisiana, 1968.

Winters, John D. "The Ouachita-Black." In *The Rivers and Bayous of Louisiana,* ed. Edwin A. Davis. Baton Rouge: Louisiana Education Research Association, 1968.

Woods, Patricia D. "The Relations Between the French of Colonial Louisiana and the Choctaw, Chickasaw, and Natchez, 1699-1762." Ph.D. dissertation, Louisiana State University, 1978.

Wright, Martin. "Log Culture in Hill Louisiana." Ph.D. dissertation, Louisiana State University, 1956.

Zelinsky, Wilbur. "Classical Town Names: The Historical Geography of an American Idea." *Geographical Review* 57 (1967): 463-95.

Parting Shot: The author documenting old plantation quarters,
Iberville Parish, 1984.